SIMPLY SANE

SIMPLY SANE

The Spirituality of
Mental Health

New Expanded Edition

GERALD G. MAY, M.D.

CROSSROAD · NEW YORK

To Betty

1994

The Crossroad Publishing Company
370 Lexington Avenue, New York, NY 10017

Printed in the United States of America

Library of Congress Cataloging-in-Publication Data

May, Gerald G.
    Simply sane : the spirituality of mental health / Gerald G. May.—
New expanded ed.
      p. cm.
    ISBN 0-8245-1366-5
    1. Spiritual direction. 2. Psychology and religion.
    3. Psychotherapy—Religious aspects—Christianity. I. Title
    BV5053.M383   1993
    158'.1—dc20   93–2581
                                         CIP

158.1

CONTENTS

PREFACE

It is a privilege for a writer to have a book published at all, but it is indeed a rare opportunity to revisit a text for a new edition after seventeen years. Written in 1976, *Simply Sane* was my first published work. Some who have read my other six books say *Simply Sane* is their favorite, and I myself have said that my other writings are just footnotes to it. It was received as I meant it to be: not as a substitute for responsible psychiatric treatment when it is needed, but as a hopeful alternative to the deadly practice of looking at ourselves as objects to be manipulated, controlled and fixed. This misconception has softened a bit in the intervening years, but it is still very much alive. A new edition makes sense.

Simply Sane holds a special place in my heart as the beginning articulation of my journey along the vague trail connecting psychology and spirituality. The basic images of the original text have never left me. Every day I call upon insights from the "True Growth and Healing" and "The Lessons of Sanity" chapters. Often I feel as if I were thinking of them for the first time. Then, when I realize their abiding truth and practicality in my life, I am filled with gratitude.

Most of all though, I am grateful that *Simply Sane* has given some real help to people. Over the years I have heard many kind words about my books and have graciously been spared the harsh criticism that many writers receive. The most gratifying responses of all, however, were from three people who told me that *Simply Sane* literally saved their lives. The book came to them at the right time, touched them in the right way, and kept them from committing suicide. I have always wanted my writing to give hope and encouragement; it is most wonderful to know that it has also given life.

In preparing this new edition, we decided not to alter the original text; to do so would create an entirely new book and many people cherish the simplicity of the original. In truth, I do not think I could really improve it. So instead of revising the old work, I have added two new chapters (14 and 15) that update and elaborate upon it. I feel a kind of tenderness toward the old words, much as I feel toward the old hand tools I inherited from my father. They are rough hewn and well worn, and they have acquired beauty by simply serving well and long. Next to them, the new chapters have a certain glitter; I hope they will wear well also.

Going over the text was like reading my old journals: embarrassing, humbling and reassuring. I was embarrassed by my early ways of self-expression: hesitancy to express my faith, triteness of examples, slips into gender-specific language, and so many sentences that lack subject and verb. I was humbled by the extent to which I still today forget and have to rediscover truths that I spelled out in such a clear, simple way so long ago. But I am reassured that such truths do abide. In relentlessly loving faithfulness, God keeps the truth coming round to us again and again. Because of this divine mercy, our essential goodness is absolutely trustworthy. That is what *Simply Sane* is all about.

I have spent the last seventeen years trying to live the truth contained in these old pages. The trying has deepened my sense of the gift-nature of faith. It is not a thing to be achieved, earned, or otherwise tried for. It comes as it is given, by the One who gives it freely, and there is little we can do except pray for the gift and for our own openness to receive it, meanwhile living as lovingly, honestly, gently and beautifully as we can. Trying is not such a bad thing. It will not achieve what we most desire, but it does *express* our desire—and that alone is an act of human beauty.

So this new edition of *Simply Sane*, old words and new, is offered to be read afresh. As the first chapter points out, new does not necessarily mean better. I have taken the opportunity of the new chapters to express myself as honestly and directly as possible. Often my statements will seem like pronouncements, as if I know the truth. I trust you not to accept what I say uncritically. Use your own sense, your own good wisdom. Read prayerfully, with wise trust, with your heart simply open to the God-given truth that abides within you.

January 1993
Shalem Institute for Spiritual Formation
Mount St. Alban
Washington, D.C. 20016

1

DEATH AND
RESURRECTION

For all things born in truth must die,
and out of death in truth comes life.
Face to face with what must be,
Cease thou from sorrow.

Bhagavad-Gita 2:27

The world is filled with newness. And it has been for years.
This new product, that new invention, this revolutionary idea.
Always something new and, presumably, better. We are a people of progress. For years the new and the novel have captured the energy of our culture. But fatigue is beginning to
set in. The novelty of novelty is wearing off.

That doesn't mean we simply want the good old days back
again. For many people, the good old days don't look so great
either. It's something else, something in a different kind of
dimension that is being sought. There is a sense that one can't
just go on forever discovering new and better things, nor can
one comfortably go back to the old. There is now a desire for
some kind of attitude, some way of perceiving existence which
undercuts and undergirds both the old and the new. Something giving meaning to the old and the new. Something giving meaning to *us*. Some way of freely, fully and *simply* being.
Nearly everyone has a nagging sense of this, for from time to
time, in fleeting moments of abandonment, *it* is experienced.
"Just being" happens. But exactly what it is or how to get it or

whether we really want it or what it might do to us if we did
get it are all unanswered questions.

So most people return to the tried and trustworthy world of
doing. The world of progress, growth, advancement, achievement and mastery. Learning things. Creating new ideas. Ac-
tualizing ourselves. Encountering penetrating insights into the
depths of individual and cultural psychology. Learning how to
become assertive. How to use and acquire power. How to
amass wealth. How to become liberated from oppression. How
to act as if we'd overcome our basic feelings of inferiority and
inadequacy. We practice hard and become proficient at the
games of politics, management, economics, security, morality,
social fitness and human relations. And we become very good
at it all.

But if by chance we have a moment with nothing to do, if
by mistake we get just a little quiet for a while, the nagging
sense comes back.

Sanity speaks in those moments.

"What for?" it says "Why?" it asks. "O. K., you've learned
and accomplished and grown. But so what? What's the meaning
of it? Where is it getting you? What is it worth?" That in-
trusive voice of sanity is most disquieting, so one tends to
move, rather quickly, to shut it up. Most of the time this is
accomplished by just becoming very busy. Busy on something
else. "I've got work to do. Can't sit around here contemplating
my navel." And if that doesn't work, one can say, "Oh, that's
just my sense of insecurity talking." One can label one's sanity
as insanity. See it as representing inadequate self-confidence,
a lack of self-esteem. Or even laziness. When that most sensible
part of ourself begins to ask, "Why are you struggling so hard?"
we can handle it by labeling it as a problem.

"Well, maybe I need a little more therapy in order to
overcome my uncertainties."

"It must be time to go on another weekend workshop to

put me in touch with my feelings. Then I will return to the world more confidently. Without all these self-doubts." Never stopping to realize that perhaps those self-doubts are the most honest, most sincere voice we can hear.

And if *that* doesn't work, if the nagging questions remain after even more work at self-improvement, then one can always drink. Or eat. Or sleep a lot. Or drug oneself in a myriad other ways. Anything to kill the nagging sanity.

Periodically, certain identifiable groups of people discover how they've been murdering their sanity. A young woman who "used to be a housewife" recently told me her experience. "For years I saw myself as Bob's wife. The mother of his children. The keeper of the house. The preparer of food. I took pride, real legitimate pride in these things. The women's lib business always seemed kind of crazy to me, and in a way it still does. But one day, when I'd watched that TV thing about being proud of your clean bathroom for the thousandth time, something sort of cracked inside of me. I mean, what was I doing trying so hard to be the wife and mother and cook, as if that's all there was? I suddenly remembered all the moments in the past when I'd felt sort of angry or depressed, and perhaps I just didn't *want* to do the dishes and I'd say, 'Hey now, you shouldn't feel that way. We all have to do things we don't want to do. What's wrong with you? Everybody else you know and respect finds great meaning in being a wife and mother. You've got to get yourself together and shape up. There's something wrong with you if you feel this way.'

"And so I'd go ahead and do what needed to be done. And I'd try so *hard* to have it make me feel good. But sometimes I couldn't get to sleep at night, and I didn't feel like I had much energy, and I'd get these headaches. Then it *really* seemed as if something was wrong with me. 'Why can't I be happy?' Well, after that last TV commercial something changed. Just because everybody else looked so happy with their clean bathrooms didn't necessarily mean *I* had to. And as time went on, it became clearer and clearer to me that what I had always thought was something wrong with me—all those doubts and resistances and stuff—was really something that was *right* with me. Now I still am a wife and a mother and a cook, but I don't feel that I have to love it all. I don't feel I must make it my nirvana. And it's O.K. to love some of it and hate some of it. And thank God, though my bathroom may be clean, I'm not in the least bit proud of it."

A very familiar and encouraging story. That kind of thing happens to many groups of people at certain times in their lives. Slaves discovered that maybe it made more sense to want to be free than to try to be comfortable as slaves. Workers found out that perhaps sanity lay in asking for their due rather than in finding ways of putting up with unfair management practices. Oppressed minorities began to entertain the idea that maybe they weren't *really* inferior. In many areas, little bits of sanity which had been labeled as insanity have become liberated.

But the sad thing about this process is that as soon as one becomes liberated from one way of stifling sanity, one tends to move immediately into another more sophisticated way of doing the same thing. The woman who overcame bathroom pride was left with a bit of a question. She never formed it into words, but it went something like, "Well, now that I know I don't have to get the meaning of my life out of being a good housewife, where *do* I get my meaning?" Lots of nice, entertaining, enticing possibilities. A career, maybe. Not noticing how men and women whose meaning lies in a career tend to have increasing numbers of martinis when they get home from work. Get rich, perhaps. Forgetting the anguish of the wealthy. Join a consciousness-raising group? Some deeply meaningful encounter with other human beings? Not even suspecting the empty pit in the hearts of those who have learned well all the techniques for relating to others in deeply meaningful ways.

And what do the "oppressed masses" do when they permit themselves not to feel inferior? They sweat, harder than slaves, forging their way "upward" into good jobs and high-class neighborhoods, wracking brains to learn how to sound sophisticated and what kind of drinks to serve and how to frequent the best restaurants. Tremendous energy to get there. And then tremendous energy to try to convince oneself that it was worth the struggle. After all, one seeks out the good life. And if one finds that one doesn't really enjoy the good life very much once it's been achieved, what is left?

The bathroom woman did join a consciousness-raising group. She went on weekend workshops where she established contact with other people. She learned how to touch them and respond to them and trust them and be trusted by them. She learned how to ask for her needs to be met, how to express her anger. She learned how to communicate "straight." And how to take risks. And each time she'd come back all warm and glowing and full of vitality, ready to tackle life with all the gusto of her being. For a while. The energy itself would last for a day or two. Then she'd pretend she still had it for another week or two. And then she'd begin to admit that she was running down a bit and that her existence wasn't quite as meaningful as she'd like it to be. So she'd say, "I'm falling back into my old patterns again. I'm still basically inhibited and not spontaneous. I need to do some more work on myself. Grow a little more. Get in touch with more of my feelings. Move along the cutting edge of my personal development."

There is a creeping insidious odor of similarity here. She might as well have been watching another TV commercial. She'd adopted another set of standards to which she felt she must adhere in order to be all right. And her natural, sensible being was drifting back somewhere far, out of sight. And she was, again, saying that there was something wrong with her.

Something needing to be fixed. Some immaturity to be out-grown. Some hang-up to be overcome.

The entire process can be very exciting and entertaining. But the problem is there's no end to it. The fantasy is that if one heads in the right direction and just works hard enough and learns enough new things and grows enough and gets ac-tualized, one will be *there*. None of us is quite certain exactly where "there" is, but it obviously has something to do with resting. As Joseph Conrad put it,

> What all men are really after is some form, or perhaps only some formula, of peace.

"There" has something to do with being able to stop all the existential struggling, and finally, just being able to let one's self be. Just to be. Fully and freely, unfettered and with wholeness. To be able to relax and be all right. To take a deep breath and lean back and sigh and *be* and have it somehow be just fine. To rest.

But always it seems this "there," this place of peace, is someplace *else*, somewhere or sometime other than the here and now of immediate experience. So in one way or another, many lives are saturated with a frantic struggle to "get there." To arrive at it. To achieve it. After I get out of college I can rest. When I land this new job. If we can just close the deal on that house. When the last kid is through school. If we can just resolve this marital problem. When my therapy is completed.

But there's no end to this kind of searching. What appears to be a destination winds up being an empty promise. There's always someplace else to go, something more to learn. And one's awareness is locked somewhere in the future, looking for the promised land that never seems to come; or in the past, saying, "Look how far I've come" or "My God how awfully deranged I used to be!" And in those very few moments when now is perceived, awareness becomes trapped in judgement. A judgement which is always made in terms of past and future. "How am I doing?" "Are they going to approve of this?" Will this get me what I want?"

And all the time there's the buried, stifled, bare potential of sanity feebly trying to ask "Why?" In the slightest of moments when this voice is heard, it is stomped out. Heavy boot grinding it back into the ground. "I must not doubt myself this way. Not so deeply. That's not what healthy, well-adjusted people do." And then one goes on to something "new."

Now and then this cycle explodes within the soul of some unsuspecting individual. Sanity bursts forth like the Phoenix and fire rains. It all comes crashing down. The point. The point of total despair. The point where giving up happens. There is no further choice. Nothing new worth doing. No more hope for the future. No more aspiration. There is some deep factor in people that makes a difference here. Something beyond the realm of predictability that determines *how* one gives up.

Some people give up *away* from life. In one last pitiful attempt to remain in control, they commit suicide. Either outright with pills or gun, or masochistically with alcohol or crime, or finally and ultimately all-in-all committing themselves to work, country, church, or value systems. It doesn't matter what form it takes. It's suicide.

But others will give up *into* life. Realizing that all the intelligence, all the learning, all the strategies, all the loving and hating and giving and taking will bring absolutely nothing, one finally gives up and lets one's self be. What we were "after" all along. What we worked for and sweated about and suffered and bled for we are finally given. But as no result of all the effort. Only as a result of having driven ourselves so far and fatigued ourselves so much that we stop the effort altogether. And then freely being is given. Not as a result of effort, but as a result of stopping the effort. Quitting.

It is a magnificent paradox. One seeks peace and fulfillment by ever-increasing effort at self-determination, self-improvement and self-control. But it is when self-manipulation and self-control are given up that peace and fulfillment are found. They were there all along.

In recent years it has become quite popular to write about the "death of psychotherapy." And in a sense this book is also about the death of psychotherapy. But it is not, I hope, another bitter attack. Nor is it an attempt to kill anything. It is rather a description of a death-and-resurrection cycle. What is dying is a mistaken attitude toward life, of which psychotherapy is but a part. A part with which I happen to be quite familiar. And what is being reborn, I hope, is sanity.

The mistaken attitude is that people have come to see themselves as things. Things to be built when they are young. Things to be fixed, altered and improved upon when they are older. Psychotherapy, along with many other cultural institutions, has fallen prey to this myth. And in its own way psychotherapy has helped to keep the myth alive. Inherent in the very idea of psychotherapy is the assumption that the human mind is an object which can and should be fixed. And that people must somehow willfully manipulate themselves in order to be "healthy." Psychotherapy has come to mean that some persons do something to other persons to fix them.

Many recent antipsychotherapy books attack the attitude of one person fixing another. They say that one person should not have this kind of power over another. They say that one should be free to fix one's self, in whatever way one deems best. But in saying this, it is obvious that the antipsychotherapy writings have also fallen prey to the delusion. They are concerned about who fixes whom. The question which still remains to be asked is "Why do we need to be fixed at all?"

There is nothing wrong in one person helping another with a problem. And there is no injury in wanting to grow or heal. The problem is that growth and healing have become building and fixing, and this distortion of reality has led us into a despairing endless struggle for self-improvement. The idea of effecting repairs and improvements upon this thing which is "myself" has so blocked our awareness of the natural processes of growth and healing that simple living has become an incredibly hard job.

But this attitude may now be dying. At this moment in time, the delusion which sees people-as-things and therapy-as-fixing is experiencing some significant symptoms of illness. There are some serious cracks in its foundation, and its death may not be far off. If death occurs, we can hope to see sanity growing from the bones of delusion. A sanity which will allow clear perception of the natural processes of healing and growth within each person. A sanity which will bring us home to our vital, dynamic, elemental roots. A sanity which will allow us to be rather than try to be; to live rather than strive to live; to be in the process of healing rather than to be the healer or the healed.

I do not advocate hastening the death of delusion by any willful means—even to put it out of its misery. Nor do I advocate wrenching the seeds of sanity from the ground before their time of birth has come. But on the other hand, if it is indeed time for delusion to die, I hope we will not take any heroic measures to keep it alive.

The current illness of self-fixing and self-building is caused by sanity struggling for rebirth. People are becoming deeply dissatisfied with the fact that in a world overfilled with self-improvement methods, fulfillment has not been found. Having tried this method of self-enrichment and that technique for personal growth, and still not finding peace, people are beginning to experience a wave of disillusionment.

As a race and as a culture, we human beings have learned so much we're beginning to wonder what the value of learning is. Many of us have become so affluent that we're beginning to wonder what it means to have power and luxury. We've been developing doubts about the importance of wealth. And we've become so sophisticated at analyzing every aspect of ourselves, our hopes and impulses, fears and faiths, that we're beginning to ask, "What for?" These questions come from the voice of sanity. And as troublesome as these questions may be, it is just possible that they will mark the beginning of salvation.

2

BEYOND SELF-CONTROL

He got the better of himself,
and that's the best kind of
victory one can ask for.

Cervantes, *Don Quixote*

Mary Jo had a sexual fantasy. It was an ugly fantasy, filled
with pain and blood. Mary Jo hated herself for having the
fantasy. She felt guilty, sinful and terribly defective. She wanted to be fixed. She could not see the *fantasy* as the problem,
but had to see her *self* as the problem because she was the one
who had the fantasy. In this, she reflected a quixotic attitude
which is civilization-wide. "I'm not happy so *I* need to
change." "I'm not efficient enough so *I* need to be improved
upon." "I'm not functioning well so *I* need to be fixed."

When Mary Jo came into my office to be fixed, I took a
furtive little stab at sanity. "Why," I asked, "do you need to
feel badly about your*self* because of this fantasy? I know it
hurts you, but is there any reason to belittle yourself because of
it?"

"Because it's me thinking it," she said, as if I'd asked a
dumb question. "Can't you do something for me to get rid of
it? Maybe hypnosis?"

I tried again. "Sure the fantasy makes you feel bad. Sure

it's a lot of trouble. But maybe if you could relax a little and let yourself be who you are . . ."

"You don't understand. I can't control it. I can't control myself. How can I relax when I can't control myself?"

There's the rub. She's laid it out clearly. She wants to be fixed so she can control herself. Her self. Once she feels she has mastered her self, then she can relax. Only then.

I succumbed to Mary Jo's conviction that self-control is the only way out, and we got into psychotherapy. On my part it was a try for second best. At least I was trying to support her attempts to control herself *by* herself and fend off her desire for me to control her through pills, hypnosis or magical medical wisdom. And, as might be expected, psychotherapy worked. Somewhere along the line the fantasy became less strong. Later it seemed to disappear entirely. But by then Mary Jo had discovered many "underlying psychodynamics" which needed to be taken care of. We were on the road, she and I. Toward the ultimate fix.

From time to time I kept trying to say, "Relax and be who you are. The fact that your impulses need to be controlled doesn't mean that you as a person have to be controlled, by yourself or by anybody else." But she didn't hear. And one of the reasons she didn't hear was because while my words were saying "Be fully, freely yourself," many of my actions were saying, "O.K., Mary Jo, let's get you fixed."

Finally psychotherapy stopped. "I've come a long way," she said. "I understand myself now. I'm stronger. I've got confidence. I'm no longer weak and helpless. Sure I've still got problems, but I can handle them. I've got control of myself now." That's where we stopped. That's where psychotherapy stops. That's even where the antipsychotherapy writings stop. That is where the entire culture seems to stop. Self-control.

The quixotic cultural myth is that in self-control, self-determination, self-direction, self-identity and self-confidence lies the good life. Nearly every cultural institution reflects this belief. There's nothing special about psychotherapy, or about antipsychotherapy, or about politics or education. All are children of the same craziness, the insanity which says self-determination is utopia. Even art, with all its possibilities for going beyond self-importance, is trampled by analysis of symbolism and refinement of technique so that "better" art can be made. And so that you and I can be "better" artists or appreciators of art. Even religion, the one great timeless gate to beyond-the-self, becomes a technique. A means to an end for self-improvement. To create better behavior, to make more abiding happiness, to manufacture holiness. There are times when through religion one comes close to turning over self-control. Offering it up. Giving up. Sacrificing the delusion. But even then, most often, it becomes the turning over of a defective self to the ultimate fixer in the sky, in the hopes of getting a rebuilt and perfected self in return. This is not going beyond self, nor is it giving up. It's using God to help one get back in control. "Thy will be done" are the words. "I will let your will be done, for now," is the meaning.

The core of this myth lies in the very idea of self. If asked to think about it, most people might say they see themselves as being made up of body and mind. And perhaps soul. Fine, so far. If one could go about life sensing that one's self is simply the name given to a particular collection of body, mind and soul, there would be no great craziness. The three parts could be seen as functioning together, influencing each other, playing out their dance of life in varying degrees of harmony.

But somehow an elaboration of this idea keeps creeping in. An elaboration which is crazy. One comes to feel that the self is something else. Something very real and substantial, which exists *behind* body, mind and soul. One senses that the self somehow "posesses" or "has" the body, mind and soul, and that it is somehow responsible for controlling them. From this rather goofy assumption, people say things like "I need to control my impulses," or "I want to improve my mind." It makes sense that impulses need to be controlled and that a mind can grow in intelligence and creativity, but who or what is this "I" which is somehow supposed to *do* the controlling or improvement?

If we were to make an object of the mind and break it into parts, it might make some sense to say that impulses, which are one part of the mind, are controlled by conscience, another part of the mind. Or that various parts of the mind control various parts of the body. But the insidious idea keeps coming up that behind mind-controlling-mind and behind mind-controlling-body, there is this "self" which somehow engineers the entire process. It might even make sense to see that the soul, a representation of some ultimate engineer, is really the self. But in action, the soul too becomes an object for the self to handle. People say things like "I wish I could get in touch with my soul," or "I need to develop the spiritual side of my life," or "My soul is thirsting for God." Who is this "I" who wants to get in touch with its soul or to develop the spiritual side of its life? Who is this "me" who possesses "my" soul which is thirsting for God? The elusive self creeps behind all things. Behind the body, behind the mind, behind the soul. Even behind our vision of God, the sense of self crawls in. God said "Thou shalt have no other gods before me." He should have looked behind Him.

Belief in "self" is far more than a simple mistake in logic or an expediency of language. It does real damage. Sensing a self which somehow possesses and manipulates body, mind and soul, these must become objects. They become *things*, and lose their wonder. Even that might be tolerable if we stopped there, but we don't. Sensing that the "self" is ultimately responsible for controlling the rest of the person, what happens when some part gets out of control? When a mistake is made?

When one fails to get what one wants? Then we begin to feel that our "self" is somehow deficient because it didn't do a good job. Then comes a veritable avalanche of delusion. If the self isn't working right, *it* needs to be controlled or improved upon. A self, which can't be found, sets out to control that very same self. Incredible, but it goes even further. When one *is* successful, when one *does* get what one wants, when things *are* "under control," who takes the credit? Who swells with pride and glory? That same elusive self. "I did a good job." Who did? "I am in control of myself." Who is?

To give credit and pride to the self somehow feels good. But of course it also sets the self up to take the blame next time if things don't go well. All serving to keep the self going. To keep it substantial. To keep it important. To keep the delusion alive. The highest values of our society have bowed to this insanity. What is more revered than self-control? Or self-determination? What enterprise holds more respect than that of self-improvement?

Mary Jo, in asking for help with her mind, was living in accordance with these values. Ideally, according to the myth, she'd have fixed herself by herself. But finding this impossible, she'd taken the next best road. She had sought out someone to fix her. She didn't simply want relief from the pain of her symptom. She wanted to become a better person. It sounds very noble. But nobility and insanity often run together, and Mary Jo's driving need for self-control is no exception.

The very words "self-control" reflect an almost indescribable insanity. Do they mean that the self is controlling some thing? Or do they mean that some thing is controlling the self? Do they mean that the self is controlling the self? Perhaps there is more than one self? A self behind the self which controls the first self? And maybe one behind that? Perhaps it is like a hall of mirrors, a never-ending series of nonidentifiable selves, reflecting each other, observing each other, and attempting to control each other? The mind boggles, of course. Because it's absolutely crazy.

How often people feel "I wish I could just let myself be." "I wish I could just be myself." "Why can't I relax and just be who I am?" These feelings are almost always accompanied by a sigh. As if people sense, deeply but unclearly, that freely being would bring relaxation, rest and peace. As if they realize that *not* freely being requires a lot of work. As if they know that *trying* to live and *working* at self-control are burdens one longs to set down. All of these perceptions are correct. They are the voice of sanity. It takes incredible effort to maintain craziness. Self-control is exhausting. And the work of trying to live saps the lifeblood of living. No wonder one longs for rest.

It is a very difficult job to grasp the steering wheel of one's life and operate all the controls when one has no real idea of who's driving, where the controls are, or even where one ultimately wants to go. But being-beyond-self-control is a very threatening prospect. Being "out of control" sounds horrifying. It seems that like Hamlet, we would "rather bear those ills we have than fly to others that we know not of." One would rather drive his machine blindly than give up the driving. The self, as elusive and erratic as it is, as untrustworthy and in need of fixing as it may appear to be, has become very precious. So precious that no matter what price "it" may extract from us, we will not let "it" go.

Mary Jo described her own fear of losing herself. "There have been times, you know, when I did let myself be. Through no special doing on my part. They crept up on me. I remember once when I was doing the dishes. Bill had gone to work and I'd gotten the kids off to school and the day was going to be my own. I had nothing special to do—just the usual routine. I started to wash the dishes, and my mind suddenly became very quiet. I watched my hands as they moved. I felt the water, was aware of its warmth, the softness of the suds. For some reason I wasn't thinking about anything in particular. I was just very brightly aware of everything. I could hear the birds singing outside, and I sensed the silence of the house. It was a beautiful experience. There was something incredibly wonderful about it. I don't know how long it lasted, but I know I suddenly got scared. Deeply frightened. And the fear killed the experience. It wasn't until long afterwards that I realized what had frightened me. It was that *I* wasn't really there. I mean I was, of course, but I wasn't aware of *me* like I usually am. I was aware of everything, and it was gorgeous, but I wasn't sensing *me*. That's what scared me." The sense of self seems so precious, is held so tightly, that even moments of ecstasy are cut short in its absence.

Humankind is now at the point where the self cannot be given up. There is no way to do it. The self cannot be killed, for it cannot be found. One may kill one part or another of one's self, but always there is another reflection, taking its place, and taking responsibility for the killing. The self cannot be willfully forgotten. Nothing can be willfully forgotten. The only way to be with one's self is to let one's self be. To accept it, as a given. A part of the human condition. Even find love for it. With acceptance and love, relaxation is possible, and one can rest for a while. And with relaxation and rest, a trust can begin to build. A trust that whatever the self is, it will take care of itself. A trust that behavior can remain responsible if one eases one's grip on the elusive steering wheel. A trust that deep and clear living happens when one ceases trying to live. And a trust that aspiration, love, caring, justice and redemption are already given. That they've been there all along, unseen because of a vision clouded by efforts at self-control.

Five Levels of Control

There are many different levels of control. Some are sane and some are crazy. One is a very basic, natural, universal

kind. Most plants will not send their roots into the air. Most
animals will not search for water in a stone. Most stones will
not roll uphill. This is the control of the-way-things-are. People
clearly share this level with the rest of the cosmos. It is simply
the way things happen.

A second level of control is that which a creature exerts
over its environment. Animals do this kind of controlling when
they build their nests or prey on other animals. People, in turn,
control animals and plants, rivers and mountains, energy and
matter. Much of this is necessary in order to live. But sometimes people get carried away with it. Sometimes the desire to
control the environment exceeds our wisdom to know what to
do with power. And serious ecological problems arise.

A third level of control is that which some human beings
exert over other human beings. It may be the kind which is
simple and loving, the kind we share with animals. Like a
mother pulling her child away from a fire. Or it may be as
complex and nasty as Nazi genocide.

A fourth level is the control which takes place within the
minds and bodies of human beings. This is the control of conscience over impulse, of decision over ambivalence, of direction over chaos.

These four levels of control are basically natural and necessary. As one moves through them, human values and ethics
become increasingly important. What gets controlled, and
how, and by whom, becomes more complex and significant.
Good and evil take on great meaning and raise very difficult
questions. What *are* we doing to the ecology? Who has the
right to control other people, and in what ways? How should
thoughts and behavior be directed? Within these four levels of
control lie most of humanity's truly sane efforts. Love and
hate, joy and sadness, aspiration and failure, creativity and de-
struction; the very meat and blood of human existence take
place within these natural, necessary levels of control. Would
that that were enough.

The problem is that human beings, intoxicated with power, try to press on. To a fifth level of control. A level which is neither natural nor necessary. A level which doesn't even really exist.

This is the level of control of the self. Control of the very being of one's life. Control of the very essence of one's existence. *To be in charge not only of what one does, but of who one is.* Humankind's movement through greater and greater levels of control created a momentum which catapulted us into the search for ultimate self-determination. Humanity seems to be saying "If only we could master this one, we could rule all, determine all . . . and then, finally, gratefully, proudly, safely, rest." The awesomeness of the task is seldom a deterrent. And failure only results in intensified effort. There is a tragic heroism to this quest. "We can handle it. If we can handle rivers and oceans, if we can handle disease and pain, if we can handle outer space and nuclear energy, we can handle anything. We can handle our selves."

The agony of the quest is that there is no end. The more that is learned, the more there is to know. And the more desire to know. The absurdity is that the struggle promises final rest and peace, but leads only into greater and greater effort.

The insanity is that in humanity's driving, arrogant search for self-control, it is searching everywhere to find its self, and its self exists only within the very searching. But humankind has made an object of everything it has controlled or desired to control, and so it feels that this "self" must also be an object. A thing. Only where to find it? How to grasp it? How to catch it?

Finally, the despair of this search, the unspoken, unadmitted awful reality of it, is that if we did ultimately discover the self and gain absolute control over it, we wouldn't have the slightest, vaguest idea of what to do with it.

There is then blessing in the midst of this agony. Our very inability to catch and control our selves is what continues to make life worth living. But why then can't we rest with that?

When Mary Jo came in to be fixed, I said, "O.K., you've got an awful problem. But why can't you still relax and appreciate your *self?* Why can't you let your *self* be? Why can't you be, with all the pain and the fighting of pain, with all the ugliness and the struggling for beauty, with all the hate and the longing for love, why can't you let your self be?"

Her voice was small and somewhat dead as she replied, "I could . . . if only I could just get in control of myself . . . then I could let myself be."

"O.K.," I said, my voice dying too, "let's see what we can do about it."

3

EVOLUTION

Then the Lord God said, "Behold, the man
has become like one of us, knowing good and
evil; and now, lest he put forth his hand and
take also from the tree of life, and eat, and
live forever . . ."—therefore the Lord God sent him
forth from the Garden of Eden, to till the
ground from which he was taken.

Genesis

It has not always been this way. Human beings have not
always felt that their selves were objects. There was a time
when people were not concerned about the self. It was a time
of simply being. It was the time after life became aware of living, but before the human will became drunk with power. In
those days human beings felt nothing special about being
human. Newborn people entered the world with no more fanfare than accompanied the hatching of a bird's egg or the
sprouting of a flower. And when someone died it was no different than a leaf falling from a tree. Nothing special.

Picture a scene, around a water hole in some warm Medi-
terranean land, where prehistoric men and women quenched
their thirst. There are hoofprints and pawprints in the mud.
Among them are the prints of human feet. There is heavy

green vegetation around the mud. The sky is clear and the breeze is warm. It is morning.

A hunched, hairy figure emerges from behind a tree and hesitates. In his hand he holds a stick, something he found in his wanderings. He sniffs and turns his eyes left and right. Sharp, clear eyes, missing nothing. Glittering eyes, open to his surroundings. Then he moves toward the water, squats beside it, cups his hands, and drinks. What can we presume is going on in his mind? Nothing special. No great thoughts. Probably no thoughts at all. Probably just crude awareness. An awareness that entertains only sights and sounds and smells and touch sensations. And the taste of the water. An awareness uncomplicated by names and judgements and plans. This human being is aware of very much. He is even aware of awareness. But he is not thinking about it at all. He is life which has simply become aware of living.

He is a gatherer, a forager, and a hunter. When hungry, he finds berries or leaves, and he eats. Or he may club an animal to death and consume its flesh. But there is no thought of eating. He may offer some of his food-discoveries to others of his kind, but there is no thought of sharing. When attacked by some predator, he may fight back. But there is no thought of defense. He senses going to sleep and waking up, but he does not label them. When something happens, it simply happens. He is not concerned with why or when or how it happens, or if it will happen again. When he does something, it is done, and there is no analysis of motivation or efficiency. He has a sense of being, but no thought of "I am."

Stand by the water hole as time passes. Perhaps tens of thousands of years. The water has dried up and come again, repeatedly. There are fewer footprints now, and the vegetation is quite different. Now it is in fairly orderly rows. At one side of the water hole is a path, leading to a small hut made of sticks and dried mud. This is the house of a farmer.

Somewhere during those tens of thousands of years people

learned that they could plant seeds to raise food rather than simply forage for it. A kind of willfulness has emerged. Humans have become able to do things intentionally to the world in order to satisfy themselves. And they have also learned to talk. No longer do they simply sense. Now the things they sense have names. And the combination of will-to-do and language has created still another sense. The sense that there is some*one* willing and doing. That some*one* is "I."

Watch now as the farmer emerges from his hut. He is less hairy and he stands more straightly than his predecessor. And though he seems to walk with more confidence, he is less acutely aware. He has less need to be, for he has now defined this land as his territory and intruders are few. But even if he needed to be as acutely aware, he could not. For now there are thoughts in his mind, and they occupy much of his attention. He is less alert, and there are some furrows in his forehead. Perhaps he has been wondering whether his crop will get enough water. He is less attentive to changes in the wind and movements in the distance. He is more secure, but his eyes are not so clear.

As he moves toward the water he thinks, "I see the water." As he bends down, "I drink . . . good." Then he takes a gourd and fills it. In his mind, "For later." As he stands to leave, he hears a sound from the other side of the water. Another human being. They look at each other, muscles tense. Thoughts follow one another quickly. "Stranger . . . attack . . . run away . . . what will he do?" But the intruder turns and leaves. The farmer's heart is pounding. "Will he come back? Are there others with him?" He stands still, straining to see and hear. For a long time. Nothing happens and slowly he calms down. He heads toward his hut.

Just before he gets there he stops and looks back. Nothing on the horizon. Nothing moving in the trees. The sun is on the water, and the farmer thinks again, "I see the water." In his simple memory he reviews what has happened. "I see the water. I drink. I fill gourd. I see stranger. Stranger goes. I see the water now. My water."

His heart is no longer pounding, but there is uneasiness in his thinking. The water is his, and he may have to protect it. It is something others want. He can't rest too easily. He is worried. But deeper than this, more insidious than this, and far more disquieting than this is a creeping horrible sense in his mind as he looks at the water. "I see the water. I am seeing the water. I drink and protect it. *I am not the water. The water is different from me.*" He feels now the pain of a basic wound. The wound of the first discrimination. The wound that was left when human thought sliced self from other. A wound which has not healed to this very day.

Already he has bought the delusion. Already he has accepted insanity. Already he carries the burden of the human predicament. To feel separate and autonomous. He feels a moment of longing, a distant memory of a time when he shared his consciousness with the water and there was no difference. No thought-discrimination.

But then he remembers he has work to do, and he must get busy or the night will catch him unprepared. So he pushes the longing, nagging emptiness out of his mind and goes about his business. He has learned to bury his sanity. Even in his simple mind the delusion is too strong, and sanity too weak.

Delusion, according to modern psychiatric definition, is a fixed mistaken belief. Something unreal which seems very real. This is what has happened to the farmer. He now feels that he is a self, separated from the rest of the world. But is he really separate? When his forebears learned to impose their wills upon the earth, when they began to think in words and sense a difference between self and other, did they really *become* separate? Did humankind really step outside the process and flow of nature, or did it just begin to feel that way?

Nothing *really* changed. There was no *real* sword which

severed humanity from the world. But it does indeed feel that way. Thoughts can sometimes seem very real.

It must have seemed to that farmer that he had once been in Eden and had now been cast out. But he didn't really leave. He wasn't really cast anywhere. Eden was, and is. He just can't believe it. Then, in moments when he notices the sunlight on the water, and when he feels a longing for reunion, he simply cannot comprehend. His sanity cries out, "Exist. Be. You are no stranger to the water. You are brothers. Simply be." But he can no longer understand. So he buries the voice. Back to work. Back to willful doing. Back to the delusion of separateness. Because now delusion seems more real than reality.

Stand by the water hole while another few thousand years pass. More people have gathered around the water, and a village has been built. More discriminations have been made. Speech is becoming refined. More things have labels. And people have become more sophisticated in willfully making and doing things. A small irrigation project has begun, plows have been made, and animals trained to pull them. Willfulness and power, becoming more sophisticated, have tended to pull the consciousness of people further into the delusion of separateness. But at this precise moment, in this precise village, an answer has been found for the nagging voice of sanity. For the time being, the people in this village are listening to their sanity.

The answer has come in the form of religion. Out of the pain of separation caused by their discriminating minds, people have made another discrimination which has a quality of healing. It is the idea of a creation. A beginning in which were fashioned, all together, the earth, the sky, water, animals and people. For a while now people can remember that they are brothers and sisters to the rest of the world. This is the pristine dawn of religion, before it became superstitious.

As we watch, a woman comes from one of the dwellings,

carrying a bowl to get some water. Her movements are slow, and she seems to be sensing the breeze as it blows across her skin. Hers is not precisely the sharp clear awareness of that first hairy creature we saw, but it is somehow more immediately sensitive than the worried confidence of the farmer. As she bends to get the water, she seems to be going through a kind of ritual. Her eyes close for a moment, and she makes some slight movements of her hands. Then she looks at the water intensely, almost devotedly, as if she were worshipping it. She gathers it up and returns to her house, careful not to spill a drop.

Her little ritual and her reverence for the water and the wind are ways of remembering her roots. She is reminding herself that she is a child of the same origins as the water, and she appreciates. Religion is born, and it serves to call the consciousness of people home. For a while, sanity is heard.

Several thousand more years pass. The water hole has dried up, and the water has not returned. Someone has dug a well. Whoever it was had been thinking, "There is something wrong here, that the water has not come back. We will fix the situation. We will dig a well and pull the water from beneath the ground." The well has produced great quantities of clear water and the village has grown. The farms now stretch for nearly a mile around. The people gather together more frequently. As we watch, we see what has happened to religion and to the voice of sanity. It is sunset.

A large number of people are gathering at the well. They are costumed and painted. In their midst, by the well, there is one man who stands out from the rest. Clothed in an animal skin, a mask on his face, he is muttering a monotone chant which neither we nor the people can understand. The people sit in an attitude of reverence. Someone lights a fire and a drum begins to beat. The man in the middle starts to dance, twirling and leaping through the smoke. As the sun goes below the horizon many of the people join the dance, and a frenzy begins to build. It lasts all night. When the sun rises again, a small animal is brought into the circle, bathed in water from the well, killed and thrown into the fire. Finally the people return to their dwellings.

Religion has changed. What had been a way of calling people's consciousness back to their roots has now become a way of trying to insure a good harvest. The idea of creation has moved to the idea of creators, powerful gods who rule over the things people cannot control. Unable to exert their will upon the wind and rains, people have invented gods who can. And now the people try to control the gods, through sacrifice and homage. Religion, once a way of listening to the voice of sanity, has fallen prey to the insatiable will of human beings to do and to control. Religion has been transformed into superstition.

If we stand by the well a few hours longer, we can see some more of the discriminations which have been made. After the nightlong ritual one man has remained by the well. All the others have returned to their houses, but this one has stayed, sitting still, like a rock. And he is staring at the sun. Later in the day, people come to the well and see him sitting there. They are puzzled by his behavior. No one else has ever acted this way. They have learned to discriminate between normal and abnormal behavior.

After a while, the medicine man is called. He approaches cautiously, walking around the sitting man, looking him over very carefully. The medicine man is thinking, "There is something wrong with this person. There is something very wrong and I am expected to do something about it. I must appease the gods when the rains do not come. I must cast out the evil spirits when illness strikes. Now I must do something to remedy this man's problem." So the medicine man begins another incantation, and he dances around the man who is staring at the sun, and after a while the man gets up and walks away.

The medicine man thinks, "I have helped this man. I have fixed what was wrong." Psychotherapy is born.

Psychotherapy was born out of the same need for control and self-assertion that changed man's wholeness into separation and religion into superstition. When the water hole dried up, something was wrong and needed to be fixed. And so people dug a well, and fixed the water problem. When the rains didn't come, people tried to influence gods who could fix the problem. And when something went wrong with some*body*, in body or in mind, someone would try to fix it. The Will of Humankind was forging its mark on the face of the earth, toward ever-increasing power, accomplishment, achievement and improvement. The world became compartmentalized into *things*, things to be handled, altered and fixed. And people became some of those things.

The small voice of sanity was heard from time to time saying, "Rest from all this struggle. Simply be." Most of the time it was ignored. On the rare occasions when it was heard, it was perceived as another problem that needed to be taken care of. Another thing to fix. And everything that was done about it helped to bury it. It could not be heard clearly and allowed to bloom because it would demand the sacrifice of delusion, and people have not been prepared to give up their insanity. No matter how painful it may be, no matter what deep suffering it may cause, the human delusion of separateness is clenched in sweating fists, gripped with white knuckles, as if it were the dearest possible possession.

This is simply the way any delusion is held. If you have a delusion that someone is plotting against you, following you with murderous intent, you will suffer continually. Perhaps you will never be able to rest, always fearing that they will be waiting around the next corner, ready to kill you. Perhaps the delusion tears your mind and destroys your spirit and makes you rather kill yourself than let them do it, but you will not give up the belief. Because as awful as the delusion is, it serves a purpose. It keeps you from perceiving something that you fear even more.

The fearsome thing we feel we must avoid by clinging to the delusion of separate selfhood is *being. Just* being. Being *without* the idea of self-determining willful control of destiny. Being *without* self-definition. That seems like death. It seems that to cease defining the self would be like nonexistence.

It feels like death. But it's not. Self-definition is simply an idea; a discrimination wound made by the sword of a thinking mind. If self-definition dies, it is no more than the passing of a thought. We fear the death of a figment.

When people do give up a delusion, if they happen to find out what it was they were afraid of underneath, they are likely to say "It was just a figment of my imagination." Precisely.

We could return to that water hole once more, in present times. There's a city there now, and the discriminations have become so numerous and complex they could not be listed. Delusion has become so deeply entrenched that sanity is seldom heard. People living in this city now laugh in scorn at primitive humanity's superstitious dances and rituals. But they're only laughing at methods. They do not laugh at primitive humanity's grinding, agonizing belief that in one way or another one can willfully control one's own destiny. They do not laugh at the idea that human beings can learn enough and do enough and fix themselves and improve upon themselves enough so that finally they will be happy. They do not laugh at the delusion. For it is their delusion as well, and ours.

But there are cracks in the streets of the city. And despair whips the corners of the buildings each morning. The people are tired. They have been searching for a way to wholeness for thousands upon thousands of years, and they are tired. They are tired of fixing and improving, and it may be that they will soon give up. Then it is possible that sanity will again be allowed to bloom. When self-definition has burned itself out.

But for the time being, the delusion goes on. And it is re-established, reaffirmed and reenacted in the growth of each child born into the human race.

4

CHILDREN

The sublimest song to be heard on earth
is the lisping of the human soul on the
lips of children.

Victor Hugo, *Les Miserables*

On occasion, and usually by accident, science creates poetry. I learned the phrase "Ontogeny recapitulates phylogeny" in freshman biology, and it has always seemed poetic to me. Even its meaning is poetic. It means that in the growth of each individual organism, the entire development of the species is reenacted. Each developing baby plays out in microcosm the centuries of evolution which have preceded it.

A human embryo begins as a single vibrant cell, much like an amoeba. This one cell grows into many, and soon the freshly forming creature sprouts a set of gills, just like a fish. Then a bit later the embryo begins to look like a salamander, complete with tail. The gills recede, turning into ears and throat muscles, the fetus grows into its tail and begins to look more human. Then a coat of downy fur grows, soft; warm, mammalian. Finally most of the fur is shed and a fully human infant is born.

This is recapitulation. The playing out of all evolution in one single human baby. But the recapitulation does not stop with physical attributes. Watching the growth of children we can see the recapitulation of consciousness as well. We can see control, self and will develop in a manner strikingly similar to that which occurred with primitive man over a period of hundreds of thousands of years. We can also watch our children learning to be crazy. Developing ways of stifling sanity. Learning to make objects of themselves. Becoming intoxicated with the morphine of self-improvement.

What is specifically human about awareness is that we are aware of being aware. I'm not sure exactly when this kind of awareness happens in the development of a baby, but I'm certain it occurs well before there is thought, and long before there is any idea of a "self" which *has* awareness or a will which controls awareness.

Some kind of awareness is present before birth. An unborn baby responds definitively to sudden movements and loud sounds. It has periods of waking and sleeping, when its awareness changes from one state to another. At birth, the infant's awareness is obvious. The baby is flooded with sights and sounds, temperature changes, pressure and pain. And it is very responsive.

Control is also present at the moment of birth. It may be hard to think of control in an infant who has yet to develop a sense of self, but nonetheless control is there. Just as it is in animals. Animals have desire for food when they are hungry, and they will control things to get food. They will control where they go, how they move and what they do in order to eat. Most of this is instinctual, but it is all a form of control in order to respond to desire. The same is true of the infant human being.

I was in the delivery room at the time of our first child's birth. Through an overhead mirror my wife and I watched the baby being born. The doctor said, "Push now, the head is coming." With the next contraction, a small, purplish, ugly, lovely head emerged. The doctor smiled. "One more contraction and we'll know whether it's a boy or a girl." We could see the baby's face in the mirror, eyes closed, expressionless. While waiting for the next contraction, the doctor took a rubber-bulb syringe and sucked some fluid from one of the baby's nostrils. The face winced. Then the doctor tried to insert the syringe into the other nostril, but the little face grimaced and the head turned to avoid the syringe. Betty and I were awestruck. Here was our child, not yet completely born and already *learning*. It was as if the baby were saying, "You got me once with that thing Doc, but you'll have trouble getting me again." With only his head born, our son was learning to exert control. In an instant, in the midst of being born, he learned that something going in the nose is unpleasant, and he tried to avoid it. Long before any idea of self or will. Long before any idea of anything.

In the hours and days immediately after the birth of any baby, control becomes much more sophisticated. A newborn infant reflexively responds to pain, hunger and cold by wriggling and crying, but soon it learns that wriggling in one direction helps more than wriggling in another. It learns that certain sounds and sights are associated with good feelings, and others with bad. It learns that crying often brings help. It begins to associate that help with a certain form, usually that of the mother. Within a few weeks the baby has learned to discriminate between stimuli, to excercise its control more efficiently, and even to some extent to distinguish its mother. Still there is no thought of this or that, no idea of self or other, no concept of desire or control.

As time goes on, the infant responds more to mother than to other people. It may cry even when nothing is wrong, just to get mother to come. It learns to mimic smiles and sounds, and to sense its own constancy while other things change. It learns that it can control its own body more than it can control other things. It learns to interact with its environment very well. And still there is no thought.

Thus far, there has been little difference between the consciousness of the human baby and the consciousness of animals. But then *words* happen. Things start to get labeled. Ideas and thoughts erupt, and the human infant begins to follow a path no other animal has trod.

With much help from parents, things start to be given names. First the "other" things. Mama, Dada, ball, toy. Then things about "me." My name, tummy, hand, toe. Then the quality of things. Nice, pretty, cold.

As the child becomes mobile, crawling around the floor, it learns an especially important word. "No." "No" seems important because it is usually associated with emphatic action on the part of the parents. A stern voice or perhaps a slap on the hand. At first, "no" is another label. This is a ball. That is a puppy. That is a no-no. But soon "no" becomes much more than a label. It becomes the very ground out of which springs the concept of self-determination. When parents simply said "No," behavior simply responded. But when parents start saying "Don't *do* that," the child begins to sense that he or she *is* somebody who should *do* the controlling of behavior. This is the beginning of a truly human self-concept.

Nearly all the messages which children get about themselves are couched in terms of what they are *doing* and how well or poorly they are controlling themselves. "You're a good girl." "You ate all your dinner." "Don't do that again." "Go to sleep now." The emerging self-image is intimately, deeply associated with doing and control. There even comes a point where the child defines itself only in terms of what it can control. And whatever seems beyond control is seen as not-self. Tripping over a toy, the child may say, "The floor bumped me." Having had an excretory accident the child may announce, "My pants wetted themselves." After sneaking a candy from the kitchen, the child may explain, "I didn't do it. My hand did."

But parents won't put up with this confusion of self-responsibility for long. They make it very clear that the child is responsible for controlling the things it does. From this point on, the child is very close to insanity. It is ready to accept the following sequence of ideas:

1. Behavior must be controlled. (True enough.)
2. There is something behind both behavior and control which is the self. (Questionable.)
3. It is that self which should *do* the controlling. (Even more questionable.)
4. If control of behavior is inadequate, then the self needs to control the self to make the self control behavior in a better way. (Absolutely crazy.)

There are times when parents sense the pain this process is causing in their children. They try to ease the little one's struggles by emphasizing behavior control rather than self-control. "I'm a bad boy," the child says. "No you're not," respond the parents. "You're a *good* boy. You just did a bad thing." But these attempts are usually weak and in vain. The child continues to equate the value of its self with the ability to control its self. The child has already gone overboard, and is well on the way to a life of self-determination.

Review for a moment how far human children have come from the animals. Desire, control, and discrimination are all present and operative in the animal world. So is learning. But without words or concepts with which to label things, a self-image never occurs. Though a rabbit may distinguish itself from a fox by running away, the rabbit never has any idea of a self which initiates or determines that behavior. Though a mother bear may exert control over her cubs by cuffing them when they stray toward danger, and though the cubs learn to control their wanderings as a result of being cuffed, there is no image of any self which is *doing* the controlling or learning. The mother bear never says "you" to her cubs. She never asks them to explain their behavior. And she never tells them to control themselves.

This is not to say that there is anything inherently better about animals not having a sense of self. Nor is it to say that human beings are flawed because they do have such a concept. There is nothing wrong with a concept of self. The problems begin when the idea of self *becomes mistaken for reality.* When the sense of self seems to become *substantial.* When it begins to seem like a *thing.* And true insanity sets in with the feeling that one should build, fix, improve upon, or otherwise control that thing.

As the image of self is developing, another concept is being formed. The concept of will. Will is another idea which begins to take on a substance of its own. The idea of will begins as soon as a child learns that it can choose to control or not control itself. A child grasps the rudiments of will from the "No's" it has heard from its parents, and from having said "No" to itself. But full and definite establishment of will finally occurs when the child says "No" to others. In saying, "No, I won't eat my dinner," or "No, I will not go potty," the child is proving how well it has learned the parental teaching that it is *somebody.* The child is decidedly and emphatically underscoring the difference between self and other, and stating in no uncertain terms that it will determine its self.

Saying "No" can be a lot of fun. Very powerful. After two years of almost total dependency and being controlled by others, the child feels fresh and liberated when he or she can say "No" *to* those others. But for the parents, it can be a bit of a rough time. In continuing to tell the child that he or she is responsible for himself or herself, the parents have made their point. Sometimes when the child is about two or three, the parents may wonder if they have not made their point too well. By this time, the question is not so much what should be controlled, but who is controlling whom.

Throughout the rest of childhood, the faculties of discrimination, control and self-determination become refined and elaborated. In adolescence, when sex hormones begin to flow and parental ties begin to break, the self takes on far more substance and importance. And a drive for self-exploration becomes evident. At times this may appear very self-*centered* and self-*ish*. At other times it may seem very altruistic and loving. But what the adolescent is doing is making a dynamic attempt to discover what the substance of this mysterious self really is.

People may ask of the adolescent "What are you going to be when you grow up?" The adolescent asks of himself, "Who am I?" Between these two questions a sort of friction erupts which makes for a very lively dance with identity. The words "What are you going to be" speak for delusion. They imply that the person is a "what," to be defined by doing. But sanity proclaims the person as a "who," evident in being.

Delusion and sanity rub against each other in adolescence, and a colorful series of experiences results. One day, identity may seem very solid and stable. On the next, the adolescent may walk about in a daze. On the following day, there may be a religious conversion, bordering on fanatacism. And on the day following that, apathy.

Delusion and sanity are at war over the self. The one wanting to grasp and determine it, the other wanting to free it to be what it will be. The one fearful of losing the self, the other willing to give it up.

Toward the end of adolescence, the battle ebbs. Dust clears from the field. Usually, delusion is the victor. Identity has been found, and sanity loses yet another battle. It loses because it has very little cultural support. Language does not give it good weapons with which to fight. Values do not hold it in high esteem, for the values of culture are often the secret agents of delusion. They say one should make something of one's self. Make some thing of your self. But most of all, sanity loses because it is not a killer. It can destroy nothing. Its only real weapon is love, and its only strategy is affirmation. And so sanity once again is covered, buried beneath the carnage of the battlefield. There it remains, constant, unchanging, incredibly simple.

Through the entire process of human identity formation, through birth and childhood and adolescence, the child is carefully watched. By educators and psychotherapists, but most of all by parents. Sometimes parents watch with awe, sensing the intricate beauty of their children's growth. Sometimes parents watch with fear, unable to know what to give their children, how to direct them. Not realizing the possibility of fully, freely being with their children, parents wonder *how* to be with their children. What is the proper technique? What is the best method? Caught in this dilemma, it is not unusual for parents to turn to psychotherapy for help. For guidance in the proper methods of raising children. And psychotherapy, it seems, always has something to say.

In its many forms, psychotherapy has offered a veritable smorgasbord of guidelines as to how children should be raised. A host of suggestions, almost all of which take the form of methods and techniques.

There was a time when psychotherapists advocated strictness, hard work and solid rules. Then, in an almost universal misinterpretation of Freud, permissiveness became the way. More recently, parents have been told that the best child-raising involves listening to feelings and straight communication. All are methods. Whether a specific method works well or not is unimportant. What is important is that parents have an insatiable hunger for methods, and psychotherapists have an unending supply. When the method is what counts, the child is lost. For methods are not used for being. Methods are used for building.

Of all the questions I've been asked as a psychiatrist, the most common and disturbing ones have been about how to raise children. It has always seemed rather strange that people can expect psychiatric training to create an authority on child-raising. It would make much more sense to search out a grandmother whose offspring are living fully and beautifully, and ask *her* about it all. But parents seem to want methods, and psychotherapy is where the methods are to be found. Complex, sophisticated methods. Grandmothers usually have only a few methods. And they're usually very simple. Grandmothers often say things like, "Well, I just did the best I could, taught 'em right and trusted in God. And I always made sure they washed behind their ears." Sane as those words may be, they're just too simple to satisfy most modern parents' appetite for techniques. Grandmothers like to see children grow. Method-hungry parents want to see children built.

The more methods we get, the more we feel like we are building our children. And the more we feel like builders, the more methods we want. Even if we use words like "raising" or "growing" rather than "building," we still feel we are doing the raising. Persisting in the belief that we are growing or raising our children, we shall continue to feel separate from them. They will remain objects for our manipulation. We will be managing their growth process rather than participating in it.

If I could now answer all the questions I've been asked about how to raise children, I'd say "I really don't know. I honestly don't know whether it's better for you to be strict or permissive, demanding or acquiescent, whether you should spank or restrict or understand. I simply do not know. Not as a psychiatrist, and not as a parent. But whatever you do, please continue to do the best you can. Just please do it in the sense of participation in growth. Watch with awe as your children's petals unfold. Marvel at the growing. Be with them in it, as fully as you can."

One of the saddest results of the "help" psychotherapy

has given to child-raising is that parents are encouraged to manipulate themselves *more* in order to manipulate their children *less*. Young mothers and fathers can be amazingly masochistic about this. Almost invariably feeling ill prepared for the job of growing children, they seek advice. From doctors and psychotherapists. Or from books by doctors and psychotherapists. Finding some specific recommendation, they often proceed to follow it even if it feels deeply wrong.

I've seen mothers crying in agony, stifling their desire to hold their screaming child because some "authority" said infants should be held for no more than an hour a day. I have seen fathers stand back while their hearts ached to respond to a child, because they'd been taught that the mother should take care of the emotional stuff. I've seen parents driven to near hysteria by the screaming tyranny of their toddler because someone had said they shouldn't lose their temper with the child. And driven to exhaustion because they felt they should never "reject" a child by saying, "Leave me alone for a while, I'm tired."

All done in love. All done with the best of intentions. Done to prevent the child from getting, God forbid, a complex. But at such a price. The price of parents interfering with themselves, of stifling who they are, of giving complexes to the *parents*, so that at some future time they might be able to say, "I did a good job raising my children." We might get a raise for doing a good job building cars in Detroit. But for doing a good job building our kids we get deeper into our delusion of separation. And the children, what do they get out of it? What do they learn by watching their parents?

I am very grateful that psychotherapy has *not* been able to come up with a sure-fire mistake-proof guaranteed child-raising method. If there were such a method, I fear we'd lose all hope of being with our children in their growing. On the other hand, I'm glad we're concerned enough about our children to worry about them. It is a big responsibility, and one has to do one's best. We have to worry about our children, and we have to suffer with them, and we have to hope for them. With all of this, it seems only fair that we allow ourselves the wonder of being with them in growth. Too often, this most precious reward is sacrificed. We sacrifice it now in the hopes of some fantasied future reward of being able to say we did a good job. Grandmothers, far more than psychotherapists, know the folly of this.

The natural growth process in children will occur. It will occur, in most cases, in spite of us. Almost no matter what we do, it will happen. We seldom kill our children by trying to grow them. What we do kill is our simple awareness of the natural growth process. Being so interested in taking credit for the growth and carrying the burden of it, we fail to see its wonder.

In those moments when we do see it—and we all have those moments, now and then, happening to glance into his room when he's sleeping, or seeing her eyes at Christmas—we can listen to sanity. In those moments we can be who we are with our children as they are. Maybe that means we'll be strict. Or lenient. Or sentimental-sweet. Or understanding. Or rejecting. It probably means that we'll be doing the very best we can in the best way we know. But we won't feel like it's all our doing. Seeing it, marveling at it, we can at the same time be an integral, active part of it.

5

THE FIX

Drink iron from rare springs;
    follow the sun;
Go far
To get the beam of some
    medicinal star;
Or in your anguish run
The gauntlet of all zones to an
    ultimate one.
Fever and chill
Punish you still,
Earth has no zone to work against
    your will.

Genevieve Taggard

By the time they reach age 21, most everyone has gone crazy a
few times and most everyone has gone sane a few times.
Enough to know the difference. But many will have decided
that crazy is the way to be, and they will be trying very hard to
make some thing of themselves.

Some will find identity by giving their lives to a company.
They will receive a gold watch at the end of twenty years and
then look around themselves and say, "Well, this is what I
worked for. Financial security. Status. Respect. But somehow
it doesn't seem as wonderful as it should."

Others will pledge their lives to the raising of healthy, well-adjusted children. Then the children will grow up and go off to raise children of their own. And there will be a time of empty loneliness. "I've worked long and given much. I'm glad my children are doing well, but what now is left for me?"

Still others will fail at what they had determined to make of themselves. They'll flunk out of school or lose the "good job" or mess up "what could have been a good marriage." Then perhaps they will try something else. If they have the energy. But it won't be precisely what they wanted, and despair will settle in.

Some of these people, the "successful" ones as well as the "failures," will just quietly stifle their doubts, make do with whatever they have achieved, and resign themselves to living through a number of remaining barren years. Others will turn about in their despair, searching for ways to regain some sense of self-control and self-determination. They may try to learn something new, take a course, seek out a new experience. Or they may find a group or a cause to which they can pledge allegiance, something with which they can identify themselves.

Or perhaps they will enter psychotherapy, seeking to find some fresh insight, understanding or encouragement which will renew their energy for self-determination. For many, this will work.

But when psychotherapy "works" in this way, it simply stifles sanity again. To a person who is approaching the point of possibly giving up psychotherapy says, "Now don't give up. There are still many ways to get back in control of yourself and of your destiny. Let me help you." Saying this, psychotherapy fans the dying embers of delusion, promising renewed vigor, new opportunity. It is deaf to the voice of sanity which is pleading, "Allow me to give up. Let me sacrifice the struggle. Allow me to accept and be, simply, who I am."

Acting as the good child of civilization's craziness, psychotherapy will recharge batteries for self-manipulation and open new doors to mastery. It will work. For a while. Until fatigue sets in again. Or until all the new doors have been entered and nothing of ultimate worth has been found behind them.

With or without the "help" of psychotherapy, some people will come to a time of ending. Having exhausted all the visible avenues toward peace and completion, being exhausted themselves, having seen every promise of fulfillment broken, some will assert the final attempt at self-mastery. The ultimate target of delusion. The ominpotence of suicide.

Most people see suicide as giving up, but in fact suicide is the antithesis of giving up. It is the final assertiveness of self attempting to control self. The ultimate challenge to being. Mastery. As abhorrent as suicide is to society, it pays the final homage to society's delusion. It is in fact the logical culmination of a life which is lived in accordance with society's belief in self-mastery.

I have said before that there are many forms of suicide. Alcohol and drugs as well as guns and pills. Slow, insidious as well as quick and definite. In attempting to destroy a self which cannot be found, suicide winds up attacking one or more *attributes* of that self. Least common but most obvious is the attack upon one's body. A more subtle but more frequent target is one's will. The will can be "killed" through immersion in passivity, subjugation to drugs, or subjugation to other people.

But suicide's most common target is awareness. The awareness which lets us know we exist. To kill awareness, to murder or drug or daze the awareness of being which is our only link with our living, is no different from murdering the "self." To kill immediate present awareness is to be dead for a while. And this is something that nearly everyone does, thousands of times a day.

Immediate awareness is killed in countless ways; in work, in play, in human relationships, in food, in worry, in racing toward success. It is no accident that one says "I lost myself," to describe the drowning of awareness in activity. Dulled, robotic, moving through life oblivious to being, we awaken to immediate living only now and then. And most of those precious waking moments become caught up in evaluation of the past or worry about the future. But it is not really our "self" which is lost in the daze of doing. It is awareness. Awareness is killed. Whatever the motivation—to rest or to get beyond the agony of self-concern—we kill the precious awareness which informs us of being. This is the way in which countless mini-suicides are committed daily.

To wake up from the daze, to come home to consciousness again, to live brightly and fully with awareness clear as winter air—this sounds wonderful. But it also sounds like a fantasy. It appears as a dream beyond human capacity. It sounds like something which would require an incredible amount of doing and an unimaginable degree of fixing. It sounds this way because we have come to associate awareness so intimately with control that it is almost impossible to conceive of one existing without the other. Being so used to evaluating and fixing ourselves every time awareness occurs, it seems difficult to conceive of being-in-that-awareness and resting at the same time. But it is not so difficult. It is no fantasy. And it takes no special fixing. It doesn't even take doing. It takes perhaps some kind of allowing, allowing oneself to give up. But not suicide. It takes allowing of relaxation, but not lethargy. It takes acceptance, but not passivity. It takes simply being. But even that seems difficult. To simply be, to fully, dynamically, energetically be, and not *do* anything about it. It seems perhaps that the delusion is too firmly entrenched and sanity too incomprehensible. Sometimes it seems impossible.

Still, there is always room for great hope. For at every level of despair there is the possibility of giving up. In the midst of every dimension of delusion there are sparkles of sanity.

For one thing, the story I have told about human growth-into-delusion does not apply to everyone. There are many people who are born with grace into this life and never accept the delusion. They never come to feel separate, and they are spared the agony of feeling that they have strayed from their roots. These people are often not very outspoken. Usually quiet and unassuming, they seldom come to public light. It is easy to forget that they exist. Still, they are many in number and can be found in the most unlikely places. In a factory in a small Michigan town, I once came upon a woman whose eyes were so clear that I could not help but feel awed in her presence. She seemed not to know this, and only smiled gently at me. On a Pennsylvania farm, an old grandfather laughed lovingly as I spoke of understanding life. He twinkled, but said no words in response to me. Instead, he invited me to help with the milking of the cows. A suburban housewife heard me discussing the difficulties of being immediately aware. "Why is it so hard," she said, "when you *are?*"

There are people like this everywhere. They simply have no great reason to announce themselves. They have no need to write, speak, teach or learn about awareness or being. Because they simply are, and their simple being says more than words ever could. These are the people whom William James called the "once born" of religion. For them, religion and living are synonymous. Being and awareness are unified. Worship and living life are one and the same thing. For them, the only "special" religious activities, the only "special" dances they perform with life, are celebration and thanksgiving. They live as best they can and accept their being at that. They do not try to do more than their best. Their behavior is responsible, but they assume neither credit nor blame. There is no need for them to try to live, for they are immersed in the process of living.

The rest of us are in James's category of the "twice born." Feeling that we have somehow come away from the essence of our being, that we have travelled somewhere off from our roots, it seems that we must *do* something to come home. Somehow we must work our way forwards or backwards to being rather than simply be. Trying to live rather than living. Fixing rather than healing. Building rather than growing. For the twice-born, religion, learning, psychotherapy and all other forms of doing are possible vehicles *to* nature. Ways of coming home.

For us, the twice born, there is great hope. At each point along the paths we follow, giving up is possible. Every footstep on the road to self-mastery represents a possibility for quitting the struggle. At the age of two or at the age of eighty, and at every point in between, giving up may happen.

In the early years of life, giving up usually takes the form of faith. A leaping forward into a belief that one is loved, accepted, forgiven and redeemed just as one is, with nothing special needing to be done. In later years, giving up more often comes from despair. From the wisdom of realizing that no amount of continuing effort, no amount of fixing, will enable one to "get it all together." Despair then is forever a doorway to life.

It must be an act of grace, or of something beyond the individual will, which enables certain people to give up at certain times. Whether the giving up occurs gradually or swiftly, with great fanfare or absolute stillness, giving up is not something that can willfully be done. It can be allowed or it can be resisted, but it cannot be done. And that is where hope lies. Not hope in continuing effort, but hope for some kind of mercy. Hope that today or next month, or five years from now there will come a time when the struggle will be sacrificed.

It seems that psychotherapy could help people realize this. It seems that therapy could be an opportunity for recognizing the possibilities for sanity in each moment of life; that it could provide space for giving up, when giving up is ready to happen. But instead psychotherapy says, "Keep trying. You can do it."

A troubled person enters a therapist's office, falls into a chair and sighs, "I'm so tired. Life is such hard work. I feel like giving up." How loving and beautiful it might be if the therapist could say, "That doesn't sound like a bad idea at all." But the chances of a therapist saying anything of the kind are a thousand to one. The therapist will panic at such a statement. He or she will have visions of suicide. And suicide would be a mark of the therapist's failure as well as the client's. So the therapist will feel, "We can't have this kind of attitude. We must do something about this." And then, the therapist will offer a fix.

There's nothing really special or out of the ordinary about the psychotherapeutic fix. There are fixes for everything in this life.

In one day's bounty of television commercials, fixes are offered for every conceivable human defect. Fixes for constipation. And for diarrhea. For runny noses, stuffy noses, ugly noses and pimply noses. For insomnia. For drowsiness. If you're bored, there's something exciting to fix your boredom. If you're ignorant, there's always something to learn. If you're not attractive enough, there's a beauty fix. There are fixes to make you smell good. There are even fixes to make you smell natural. And to make your hair curly if it's straight and straight if it's curly.

In all kinds of advertising, from the blatant affront of TV commercials to the subtleties of word-of-mouth, nothing can escape the fix. And it's not just that fixes are *offered*. The message also is that one "ought" to be fixed. That if perchance one should pass a certain fix by, not partake of its wondrous possibilities, one really isn't being very responsible for one's self.

Our attitudes toward this fix-pitch are very interesting. On the one hand, there is a strong desire to be fixed. On the other, there is a feeling of being insulted by the suggestion that we *ought* to be fixed. It is not too difficult to accept that one's house, automobile, clothes or sewing machine need to be fixed or improved upon. And it is without great discontent that one might learn that there are better ways of washing dishes, laundering clothes or fertilizing the lawn. But it becomes more irritating to be told that one should fix the way one's body smells, the way one wears one's hair, the form and substance of one's breasts, the configuration of one's hemorrhoids or the water level in one's sinuses. As the suggestion of fixes approaches closer and closer to one's sense of "self," one tends to become more insulted. Suggestions as to how one should behave, or feel, or what one should aspire to, come as more of an affront to human dignity. But in spite of the insult there is always a market for the fix.

Pills, liquids, understanding, knowledge, do your body this way or that. Change your food, change of scenery, change behavior. If the child is hyperactive—energy fix. If lethargic—stimulation fix. When worried, do an anxiety fix. When depressed, a happy fix. Having marital problems? Marriage fix. Sexual difficulties? Sex fix. Too shy and self-conscious? A confidence fix. Can't say no and stand up for your self? Assertive fix. Feel weak, vulnerable, abused in life? Power fix. Poor? There's a way to get money. Feel a gap between yourself and your children? Communication fix. Understanding fix. Alienated? Meaningless? Wondering what it's all worth? Spirit fix. Religion fix. Buy this belief. That technique. This prophet. That guru. And be happy. Obsessed? Entranced? Hallucinating? Preoccupied, impulsive, confused, despairing, suicidal, want to kill somebody? Mind fix. Be well adjusted. Analyze, free-associate, express feelings, get in touch, reenact, work it through, understand, relate, scream it out, live it out, act it out, transcend, integrate and become whole.

From ghettos to pollution and from impotence to domination there is a fix for everything. Why then, one might ask, is humankind still so troubled? The usual answer to this question would be that we just haven't found quite the *right* fix yet. Or that we haven't been fixed quite *enough* yet. Or that not quite enough people *want* to be fixed yet. Always the problem seems to be somewhere in the method. Yet there's nothing especially wrong about the methods. Except that they are seen as fixes.

Looking back over history, it seems there may be another reason why all the fixes haven't been able to fix us to our satisfaction. It appears that the more fixes that are discovered, the more there is to be fixed. With each improvement the more there is to be improved upon. The unending river of fixes continues to branch and branch, forming countless tributaries, innumerable swamps, but never reaching the ocean. You can make your own analogies between this and the fix of the drug addict. Sometime, at some point, sanity will have to ask, "How long will this go on?"

Learning teaches us only how ignorant we are. Which would be beautiful if ignorance could be accepted. Power teaches us only how weak we are, which would be fine if weakness could be affirmed. The discovery of new fixes teaches us only how much in us is imperfect. Which would be superb if only imperfection could be loved. If only imperfection did not always have to be fixed.

There is a tree outside my window. One half of it is full and green. The other half was struck by lightning many years ago. The gnarled, empty branches of this half frame the spring leaves of the other. Do I call it deformed, inadequate, in need of surgery because it is not perfectly round and full? Its imperfection is its beauty. Its imperfection is its perfection.

Human beings might recognize the beauty of an imperfect tree. But human beings can no longer see themselves as natural and beautiful in their own imperfections. Not when fixing offers perfection. It is easy to love imperfection in nature, but not in ourselves. Fix we must, and the fixing requires more fixing . . . .

To say that this leads to alienation is mild. It leads to much more. Alienation is a wandering emptiness, dry, lifeless, barren. There is a quality of quiet to the despair of alienation. But modern society is dynamic, driven, relentlessly striving, very noisy. There is more than alienation in this. There is a deep propulsion to *do* something about the human condition; a chasing and racing after something somewhere which will make it all better. A challenge to conquer alienation. To master despair. People are propelled by the belief that continually increasing effort, more and more sweat, more and more noise, will finally bring peace.

It is beyond this agonizing struggle for self-improvement, beneath the endless fatigue, that alienation turns malignant. With the feeling that people are unnatural. All living things grow, heal, develop, and do what needs to be done to live. But human beings are the only creatures who try to improve upon their very selves. And this leads to a pervasive sense that anything created by humankind is somehow artificial and contrived.

Sensing the choiceless insanity of their compulsive attempts at fixing, people look upon "nature" as very distant from themselves. The more we continue to wreak havoc upon the ecology of nature, the more we ache with nostalgia at the thought of wilderness untouched by people. On the one hand there is compulsive driving to improve upon nature, and on the other a deep sense that what is natural is better than what is manmade. The illogic of this is to be expected, and its humor is not surprising.

In the midst of fixing and improving upon nature we long for untouched wilderness. There seems to be an air of pristine purity about something which has been "untouched by human hands." As if our hands were dirty. There is a quality of freshness about a place "where no man has set foot." As if our feet inflict wounds upon the ground. We speak of "virgin forests" as if a kind of rape took place with the entrance of humankind. Looking at the untouched beauty of newfallen snow, one sometimes wishes human footprints would never mar its surface. But the prints of animals seem only to add to its beauty. So at times we feel like interlopers on the planet earth. And very often, we feel like strangers in our own homes.

Untouched forests and newfallen snow are, according to human discrimination, part of the nature which is *outside* us. But we have also come to feel distanced from the nature *within* us. There is a sense of being-ness deep inside which often seems very far away. Whenever one speaks of wanting to "just be" or to "relax and be myself," that is an expression of longing for *inner* nature. The desire for a way of being which is as pristine and fresh as new snow. It lies, we feel, somewhere beyond or beneath all the self-manipulation and improvement. The dilemma is that it always seems to be somewhere other than here, sometime other than now. It is perhaps Eden, the garden from which we were cast because of our knowledge. But there is no distance between the time or place of Eden and our immediate consciousness. Eden is. One need not travel to get there. One need not do anything to get there. But that is very hard to do.

6

DISCUSSIONS WITH TWO PEOPLE

We are healed of a suffering only
by experiencing it to the full.

Marcel Proust

CARLA

Carla was, and is what is known as a "facilitator." A leader of
human growth groups in which people build and fix themselves. One day she spoke to me of feelings. She had learned,
she thought, that in order to be whole one should express one's
feelings. So every time she had a feeling she would express it.
And it would be "worked through," understood, and integrat-
ed.

"God, I'm tired," she said. She explained that her marriage, her family and her friendships had become so complicated and out of control that she felt about to collapse. She said,
"This morning I asked my husband a question, and he turned
his back on me. I thought he was shutting me out, and I told
him how it made me feel. But he just exploded. He said he
only wanted to get something out of the refrigerator and why
did I have to take everything so personally. Then we got into
this big fight. Ah, we eventually got it worked through, but
. . . you know I just wonder if we'll ever get enough worked
through, so we can just be together."

I asked a simple question. No special insight intended. Just curious. "Why did you need to tell him how you felt?"

She looked at me, surprised. She opened her mouth as if to say, "What do you mean? How can I have a feeling and *not* express it?" But the words never came. Her mouth just stayed open, for a long time, and then she started to cry. Great heaving sobs, her shoulders shaking in spasms.

I had no idea what was happening at first. After a while, she stopped crying, looked at me and very quietly, slowly said "I thought . . . so long . . . that I *had* to, *must* tell people what I felt. Like I'd be dishonest if I didn't . . . or I'd be repressing something . . . it never occurred to me just not to say something I felt."

She went on to say that as a child she *had* stifled the expression of many of her feelings. She *had* been repressing them, and there were many times when she *had* been dishonest about them. Then she had some therapy and began work in the human potential movement. Encounter groups, sensitivity training. In this process, she felt, she had fixed herself. She learned to stop repressing and to start expressing. And she felt liberated. For a while. Until the expression began to create more problems than the repression had. The fixing had created more things that needed fixing. That was how she came into therapy with me. Of course the therapy was more fixing.

I hadn't meant, when I asked about her expression of feelings, that she needed more fixing. But after her learning, healing, calming realization that everything did not have to be expressed, she did begin to see another fix on the horizon.

She said, "I need to learn *not* to express so much. That would be such a relief." By then I was caught in the fixing too, for I agreed with her. But in my heart was the question, "O.K., when we get that fixed, what will be next?"

There came a time in Carla's life when she began to take it easier on her self. For a long while, she saw this as the final fixing she had always needed. But slowly she began to give up even that idea. I don't know whether it was from fatigue or realization, but she began to give up. There was no great insight. No breakthrough in therapy. But she seemed less interested in improving upon herself and more excited with the process of living. Once she said to me, "It's not really that important . . . I mean the way I live my life is not really that important if I just do the best I can . . ." And then she started to laugh. Big hearty guffaws. "It's the most important thing in the world, how I live, but it really doesn't matter! Because I'm going to do my best at living, and I couldn't do more than that anyway, could I? I mean, I've put all this effort into making my best better. That's crazy. How can I do that? Popeye said it right. Popeye has it all together. 'I am what I am and that's all that I am,' that's what Popeye says." We both collapsed in laughter. Somehow she had been able to begin giving up, and I was privileged to share her celebration. A celebration of a just-beginning restfulness.

JOE

Joe was, and is, a therapist. He'd had a lot of therapy himself, and he didn't come to me for "help" with any problems— we were simply friends sharing our thoughts and hopes. Joe has a strong sense of the religious aspect of his life, and he has a deep belief that there is a creator with whom communication can take place and in whom everyone's being is given meaning.

One day Joe told me, "My faith in God makes things tolerable. Sometimes even beautiful. It's helped me make it through lots of rough times . . . when I'm sure I would have crumbled without it. But my faith should let me rest. I mean it should be a way of knowing, underneath, that things are basically all right. I should be able to rest in that, but I can't. All my faith does is tantalize me . . . tease me with the possibility that somehow . . . you know, sometime, someday *maybe* I'll be able to really relax."

He went on to describe himself as a "workaholic" who could never quite relax as long as there was some need left to be filled, some knowledge left to be learned. He compared his need-to-do with hunger. "I'm stuffed. I feel stuffed . . . but I'm still hungry. Like I've crammed myself full of doing and responding to things and learning things and coping with things. Like I gobble up every challenge that comes along. I'm stuffed, but I'm still eating everything in sight. Maybe someday I'll explode."

For him, work and achievement really were like eating. He had a feeling that maybe the next job he ate, the next task he chewed up, the next knowledge he digested would finally satisfy him. But it never did. And the more he ate, the more things there were to be eaten. And he never knew which one would finally satisfy his hunger and let him rest.

"I have a friend," he said, "who used to be just like me. Going, going, looking for the big thing to do to fulfill himself. *He* had a heart attack. I went to see him in the hospital. He was lying there and he had this peaceful smile on his face. He told me, 'Now I can rest, Joe. I have to. I don't have any choice.' Now he's fully recovered and he's doing just fine. You know, he's still doing a lot. He's still a real dynamic, energetic guy. And he's still very successful . . . but somehow he's also resting. Underneath. Like though he keeps doing a lot, the doing isn't so important to him. It isn't *everything* to him. He's not all caught up in it. He's just being himself, and he seems very peaceful about it. Now how come *I* can't do that? While I still have a choice? What do I have to do, stuff myself to death before I can rest?"

As I remember it, our discussion ended there on that day.

Both of us had the feeling that we wanted to move ahead and try to come up with something he could do to ease his dilemma. But in the same moment we also knew that anything we might suggest would just be another thing to do. Another fix. Another piece of work-food for him to cram into his already bloated being. So we were silent. We sat right through the desire to say something or suggest something or even hope something. And toward the end, just before we got up to leave, we both felt a little peace. Just a hint. Too delicate, it seemed, even to express it.

On another day, Joe told me the following story. "I had to give a talk on behavior therapy to the professional association last night. You know what happened? I'd really been worried about the talk. Like how well I'd do, and whether they'd be interested in what I had to say and stuff. I stewed about it like I stew about most everything. I started to sit down and write the whole thing out, get it prepared just right, but I got to feeling just sick of it. I said 'To hell with it. I'm not going to bust my back over this one. There's too many other things to worry about. If I do O.K., I do O.K. If I don't, I don't. It's not life or death.' So I just relaxed. And I went in there with about three sentences written down and I spoke off the cuff and it was the best damned speech I ever gave. Even *I* was spellbound by it."

Even though he was speaking about something which had gone very well for him, he seemed sort of angry as he talked. As if he were feeling the injustice of all his needless struggling, angry with himself for knowing the value of letting be, even knowing how, but being able to "do" it only on rare occasions.

He continued, "It all went just beautifully. They all said how good the speech was, and afterwards I was driving home, feeling really good and peaceful. That's when it happened. Things started to change. I watched it this time and I know just what happened. I had this good, warm feeling. And then a thought came. Like 'Boy, I sure handled that well.' See, that was a kind of pride or something. Which would be O.K. except it wasn't anything I really could take credit for. I mean, if I just relax and let be, I can't really take credit for the good stuff that happens, can I? I can feel good about it, sort of celebrate it, but I can't really take credit. Anyway, I *did* start to feel proud about it. And that set me up. I can see just exactly how it happened. The first thought was 'I did a good job.' Then the next thought, right on its heels, was 'Yeah, and I hope I can do as good a job tomorrow . . . when I have that important interview or something.' You see? And then all the peace and celebration just evaporated and I was stewing again."

Joe said he knew, intellectually, that he both functioned better and felt better when he could relax and let himself be, but for some reason these letting-be times occurred only frequently enough to tantalize him. He couldn't put it into continuing practice. Of course that's because it can't be *put* into anything. It can't willfully be *done*. But Joe tried.

One way he tried was to say "To hell with it" more often. But pretty soon he found himself getting lazy that way. It didn't work. He realized that saying "To hell with it" wasn't letting himself be. It was stifling that part of himself which needed to work and achieve. No matter what he *tried* to do, he couldn't let himself be. He was always pulling on one side of himself and pushing on another. He became very frustrated. Letting himself be had become another task to tackle. Another thing to be mastered. And this was one he couldn't pull off.

Finally he sighed and said, "I've always known I was obsessive-compulsive. I thought I'd gotten rid of most of that in therapy, but I guess I haven't. I'm just a compulsive nut." He smiled a little as he said this, but the smile was not humor. I knew what he was thinking. He was wondering if he needed more therapy. And he was feeling very tired. He began to cry then, and I did too. We both knew that therapy too would be just another thing to do. But tired as he was, Joe couldn't shake the feeling that there was something wrong in him, and that he needed fixing, and that the fixing would take a lot of work.

I told Joe how I shared the very same kind of pain. We spoke of how millions of people share it, having such great difficulty in letting themselves fully and simply be who they are. How men and women all over the world are caught up in trying to improve themselves, make themselves different or better than they are. How the bionic man is the hero of our times, the man who was rebuilt, made better than he was.

Finally Joe said, "If I could only draw a line somewhere. If I could say, 'sure I need to do this well, and sure I have responsibilities, and sure I can improve things about myself,' but if I could just draw a line somewhere between improving things *about* myself and improving my *self*. If I could just finally say, 'I will work very hard on this and that, but here is me and me I will let be.' If I could just draw that line, I think I would be able to rest."

Joe never sought out more psychotherapy, and he didn't have a heart attack either. But he is more relaxed now. There was no great illuminating realization—no breakthrough into being. But somehow, perhaps through repeatedly seeing the crazy humor of his bind, he gradually began to relax.

The most significant realization he had was that in order to relax he had to allow himself to be tense. In other words, he recognized that he was a tense, driven person, and as long as he was trying hard to relax he was just increasing his tension. He finally found himself saying "O.K., I'm tense. That's part of who I am right now. So I'll just let me be." And almost in the very saying of this, in the simple act of giving himself permission to be who he was, he would begin to relax.

As the months passed, Joe continued to get caught up by worries and struggles and striving. But there was a difference. He'd found a sort of "place" from which to view it all, laugh gently at it, and give it permission to be. So that underneath the tension, he was beginning to relax.

When we talked recently, Joe still described himself as being "a long way" from his ideal concept of how he should be. But he could see himself growing and healing, and he was willing to let that process take place at its own rate. He put it this way. "My body still gets tense. My mind still gets obsessed with needs to do things right. My emotions still get hooked by success and failure. But *I* am relaxed."

As he saw it, there were two levels in his being. One was the rather hectic day-to-day level of necessity and accomplishment. In this level he needed to respond to the world around him in an energetic way. There were mouths to be fed, people who needed help, a society needing his full participation, and a world he hoped would be somewhat better because of his presence. But underneath all of this, Joe felt there was another level, one he called "existential." It was a level in which he could appreciate his being. He could be anxious and driven in the day-to-day level, but still relax at the existential level. That's what he meant when he said, "Underneath it all, I can still relax."

When I asked Joe about what was happening to his religious faith, he paused for a long time. Finally he said, "It's still there. More so than ever, I guess. But I'm not *using* it so much. As I think about it, I guess I had been using it as a way of coping with stress. It was a kind of tool to help me live. That's changing now. I can't quite put my finger on it, but it's like . . . well . . . I'm not leaning on it so much. It's becoming stronger but more diffuse at the same time. I feel its presence more and more . . . but it's harder to describe what it is. Sometimes I feel as if it's sort of replacing me somewhere down deep. And that scares me a little. But at the same time I trust it. I don't know . . ."

I suppose that this is just the very beginning of healing for

Joe. It is just a tentative budding of sanity. He still clings to a solid image of a "me" somewhere behind all the attributes of himself. And he still is compartmentalizing his being into different dimensions and levels. But that's just fine. No doubt his sanity will be quite different from my perception of it. But mainly he has quit trying to fix himself. Whatever that "me" behind everything is, he's letting it be. He'll let it be what it is, even if it does turn out to be nothing at all. He's realized that whatever the "me" is, it is beyond his power to catch it and mold it. So he can relax. And as he relaxes, "me" becomes less important. Joe is healing, I think. Not healing himself. Not being healed by anybody else. Joe is simply healing.

7

PSYCHOTHERAPY

Within my earthly temple there's a crowd.
There's one of us that's humble; one that's proud.
There's one that's broken-hearted for his sins,
And one who, unrepentant, sits and grins.
There's one who loves his neighbor as himself,
And one who cares for naught but fame and pelf.
From much corroding care would I be free
If once I could determine which is Me.

Edward Sandford Martin, *Mixed*

Throughout this book I have used psychotherapy as an example of the fixing-delusion which now pervades nearly all of our
civilization. Carla and Joe are examples of psychotherapists,
but they are also simply people. People who like thousands of
others are suffering the pain of dying into sanity.

Psychotherapy as an art and science has been suffering the
very same kind of agony. It too is in the process of dying-to-be-
reborn. Its very identity as the mind-fix of mankind is gasping
what appears to be the last breaths of life.

The mortal wound of psychotherapy occurred when it
made objects-to-be-fixed of the people it was trying to help.
Exactly when this occurred is lost in history, but for generation
upon generation psychotherapy has been caught in a self-im-

posed maze. Feeling that it must fix something, it has been endlessly searching to specify exactly what that thing is. In the 1800s, psychotherapy tried to fix the brain. Early in the 1900s, it tried to fix the mind. More recently it has gone after behavior, relationships and consciousness. Even the human soul. Trying to step back into the role of the priesthood, psychotherapy may have completed its life cycle. Attempting to objectify the human soul may have been psychotherapy's suicide.

An elderly man once told me, "Watch who is the hero in popular jokes and cartoons, Jerry. You'll see that they're all about who seems to hold the greatest hope for mankind. When people feel their hope is in religion, the jokes will be about priests. When psychotherapists promise salvation, *they'll* start appearing as the heros of jokes and cartoons."

Sure enough, when I was a youngster in the 1940s, many of the popular jokes were about clergymen. This was the age of the "Did you hear the one about the priest and the rabbi?" jokes. Then in the 1950s, the hero began to change. Slowly the priest disappeared from the cartoons, to be replaced by the psychoanalyst. The clerical collar was gone, to be replaced by a beard, a Viennese accent and a couch. Then people were asking each other, "Did you hear the one about the guy who walked into the psychiatrist's office?"

In the '60s, the clergy began to feel that psychotherapy was perhaps the only way to offer "real help" for people. Many of the clergy were feeling that the church wasn't accomplishing much. So they left. In droves. Some to immerse themselves in social action. Many to chase the hopeful star of psychotherapy.

As all this was happening, I was training to be a psychotherapist. When I started practice, directing a drug abuse program in a small Pennsylvania town, there were many clergypersons around who were busy learning psychotherapy. I helped teach them. But at the same time I was also learning that my psychotherapy wasn't really helping my clients. They'd solve their neuroses. They'd fix their personality problems. But underneath all the improvement they still seemed empty.

Many of those who were addicted to drugs remained addicted, even though it appeared that their "psychological" problems were getting resolved. Those who did go on to a drug-free life, a life filled with meaning, were candid enough to let me know that their transformation had little or nothing to do with my therapy. They explained that what had made the difference for them was some kind of deep spiritual, existential experience. An experience which went far beyond their bodies and minds and somehow got them more interested in being and less interested in *how* to be. I recognized the spiritual basis of these kinds of transformations, so I asked my clergy colleagues for help in understanding it.

But by then my clergy colleagues were immersed in psychotherapy and their answers came straight from Freud. "Well, maybe it's a change in cathexis, a primary narcissistic experience, or perhaps some displacement of Oedipal feelings," they'd say. Then it began to dawn. Here I was, a psychotherapist suddenly wanting to become a priest, in the midst of priests who wanted to become psychotherapists. There's a lesson here, and it goes deeper than that the grass is always greener. The lesson is that an accurate perception of reality lies beyond *both* traditional psychotherapy *and* traditional religion.

The same kind of paradox can now be seen in the newest field of psychotherapy: transpersonal psychology. The transpersonal school has grown out of psychotherapy's chronic inability to go beyond a person's autonomous ego, to a deeper, more spiritual level. Transpersonal psychology is the up and coming thing in psychotherapy right now and it relies heavily on mysticism and Oriental thought. As a matter of fact, American culture as a whole has become very interested in the mystical secrets of the Orient. See who seems to offer hope for humankind now. See who's in the cartoons now. The Guru. The Yogi. The Swami. But the relationship between West and East is strikingly similar to the relationship between clergy and psychotherapists. Americans, tired of technology, scientific productivity and materialistic leisure are turning to the Orient, seeking the key to a peaceful spirit. And what is the Orient doing in return? Gobbling up the technology and scientific productivity of the West, seeking the key to materialistic leisure. Again, the lesson here is deeper than that the grass is always greener on the other side of the Pacific. *Neither* East nor West has the answer. Because the answer is not something anyone can possess.

Once more I must underscore that the defects or changes we can identify in psychotherapy are not the special *fault* of psychotherapy. They are simply reflections of culture. And not even just Western culture. It doesn't seem to be anybody's special fault. It's more like a huge cosmic joke being played on all humanity. I cannot help but understand Robert Frost's prayer that if God would forgive the many little tricks "I've played on Thee, then I'll forgive Your great big one on me."

It is indeed humorous to see psychotherapy in its recent history, chasing the elusive self across the wilderness of human experience. Trying to find it, hold it, study and fix it. In the eighteenth century, psychotherapy tried to catch the self by ordering it to bow to the commands of God's morality. ". . . the affectations of the heart . . . must spring from a chaste mind and . . . Christian piety" (from an 1801 description of Burton's *Anatomy of Melancholy*). In the nineteenth century, neurologists moved in upon the brain. The pineal body, a little nubbin at the base of the brain, was felt for generations to be "the seat of the soul."

Around the turn of the twentieth century, Sigmund Freud

pulled psychotherapy away from both religion and neurology and focused on the *functions* of the human mind. Freud saw religious activity as mere displacement of sexual and aggressive instincts and he tended to feel rather threatened by things bordering on the mystical. Thus though Freud kept a healthy respect for the field of neurology, he turned his back on religion.

It seemed to Freud that the self could be examined in terms of how it functioned and the energy it used. In the 1920s, he came up with his famous "Structural Hypothesis" of id, ego and superego. While claiming that these "Structures" were concepts and not real things, Freud and his followers nevertheless began to relate to them as if they *were* real. They spoke of something being *in* the ego, or energy coming *from* the id. In this, the Freudians simply bought the age-old human delusion of seeing the self as an object. They just gave it a different name.

The tributaries of Freud's great knowledge went on to try more clearly to define the human mind and self. Adler conceptualized the self as a unity of personality and stated that infants start from a position of inferiority and strive for superiority and "self-realization." Rank emphasized the importance of the human will in separating self from other. Sullivan saw the self as a "system," a technique for avoiding anxiety. Horney spoke of a triple concept of self, including "actual" self, "real" self, and "idealized" self. Assagioli spoke of a personal self and a higher self. People started distinguishing between the self with the little "s" and the Self with the capital "S." Phrases like "self-realization," "self-actualization" and "self-awareness" became very popular. The idea sprang forth that one could be separated and alienated from one's self. (Without great consideration of who it is that is alienated.) And it was assumed that one should look somewhere to find one's self. (Without great consideration of who it is that is looking.)

There were real selves and false selves, good selves and bad selves, unfulfilled selves and completed selves, solid selves and diffuse selves.

In the midst of this gaggle of selves, behavior therapists labeled the self as a repertoire of behaviors and then gently set the whole idea aside. They should be commended for this, for of all the schools of psychotherapy, the behaviorists are perhaps the least likely to try to meddle with one's soul. The existentialists also set the idea of self aside, in the name of phenomenology. No preconceived ideas. They did go ahead and try to meddle with it but at least they admitted having no way of knowing what it was they were meddling with. Scanning the pages of twentieth century psychotherapy, one gets the impression that there are little selves running all over the place. Yet each remains incredibly elusive. Nowhere has the self really been found.

There is great value in all this work on self. It is a probing into delusion and it carries the merit of negative findings in research. One can learn as much from what is *not* found in a scientific investigation as from what *is* discovered. What has not been found is the self.

Perhaps there are bodies, senses, behaviors, thoughts, feelings, memories and hopes which can be willfully modified. But it looks as if psychotherapy will not find a self to modify. If a self exists, it is lying somewhere beyond our touch, unknown, incomprehensible, indefinable. Perhaps it is as ineffable as God, as inexplicable as the cosmos. And if it is to be fixed in any sense, perhaps it will have to be God or the cosmos that will do the fixing.

One might have hoped that this realization was what accounted for the new transpersonal school of psychotherapy. But I fear this may not be the case. Some of the giants of psychotherapy, often toward the ends of their careers, have alluded to the need to go beyond objectivity and self-fixing. Jung was especially notable in this and many transpersonalists try hard to follow in Jung's footsteps. But all too much of transpersonal psychology reeks of being simply another wave of delusion. Rather than to fix brain or mind or even self, much of transpersonal psychology wants to fix consciousness. Again, I fear these are simply new names and new techniques for the same old insanity.

I remember the day I became a transpersonal psychotherapist. I was approached by a young psychologist who had heard of my interest in meditation, spiritual awareness and such. He asked me to speak at a symposium as a representative of "my field" of transpersonal psychology. This struck me as interesting and a bit reassuring. There had been a time when I was "Freudian" and then I was "eclectic" for a while and then "sort of an existentialist." But after my experience with trying to treat drug-addicted people, I hadn't been at all certain what I was. So for a while I became a transpersonalist. Problems began immediately. I was expected to present transpersonal ways of fixing people's difficulties. To lay out the great transpersonal smorgasbord of meditation, psychedelics, biofeedback, Eastern mysticism and assorted condiments, each with its specific goals and techniques.

I should have known better, but the temptation was too great. I should have realized that in defining myself as *anything* I could not help but objectify myself, the people with whom I worked and the ways in which we worked together. There is a seductive security in identity-making, just as there is security in any delusion. But there is also despair. I am no longer a transpersonalist. One sometimes wonders how many identities will have to die.

Psychotherapy now faces the very same dilemma that every individual human being has faced throughout history. It must die to be reborn. It must lose itself in order to find itself. It must be willing to sacrifice its entire identity if it is to follow the path toward sanity. It must be willing, as must each person, to sacrifice power, self-definition, self-manipulation, and self-determination. Psychotherapy must sacrifice any idea that it does healing. And since this is its basic identity, psychotherapy, as we know it, will die.

The time seems right for this death and resurrection, but it might not come to pass quite yet. It may well be that the possibilities which transpersonal psychology has to offer will be turned toward greater and greater self-power. To more fixing. This has already happened in many spheres. How many people use meditation as a way of increasing their private efficiency and success? How many seek contact with other planes of consciousness in order to have some experience or develop some ability which will make them special? How many therapists use meditation, biofeedback or psychedelic drugs to fix, improve upon or otherwise "alter" the consciousness of their clients?

All these things are happening. It is to be expected. But what is unknown is whether that is *all* that will happen. Whether the wealth of mysticism will *only* be turned to the self-fix. Or whether at some point psychotherapy will finally give up. Again, the situation of psychotherapy is the same as yours and mine. It is possible that giving up will happen. Some way, sometime and perhaps soon, it just may happen.

8

TRUE GROWTH
AND
HEALING

Nothing prevents our being natural
so much as the desire to appear so.

Francois, Duc de la Rochefoucauld

If psychotherapy as fixing does die, perhaps the rebirth of
sanity will reflect a realization of what true growth and healing
really are. Delusion leads one to assume that growth is building and that healing is fixing, but what really is the nature of
growth and healing?

It will be difficult to specify this, for to do so will tend to
make objects of growth and healing, and they are not objects.
It may also make growth and healing appear as things-to-be-
achieved, and they are not. Still it is perhaps worthwhile to try
to describe some of the aspects of true growth and healing. It
might help us to recognize them, and perhaps appreciate
them, when they occur.

Basically true growth and healing are neither events nor
interventions. They are processes. Processes that happen. Look
at growth first.

GROWTH

True growth is a process which one allows to happen rather

than causes to happen. A seed grows into a plant because it is its nature to do so, not because you or I *do* it. If a seed finds itself in rich earth, with reasonable quantities of water and sunlight, growth will happen. If we sprinkle the ground with fertilizer, water it regularly and keep pests away, we become involved in the growth process, and growth may be stronger and richer. We are participating in the growth, but we are still not doing it.

But if we were to be displeased with the speed of growth, and if we were to dig up the seed, pry it apart and attempt to pull the young sprout forth before its time, we shall have gone too far. In trying hard to do the growing, we can actually interfere with the process. Then perhaps the seed will die.

In tending and nurturing a flower, we may be participating harmoniously with the rest of nature in the flower's growth. But if we try to pull the petals apart, we overstep. In the one way, we are participating in the process of growth. In the other, we are trying to *make* something. It is in this trying to *make* that one begins to feel separate. The thing being made becomes an object, different and distanced from the maker. Then perhaps the maker will begin to feel unnatural.

More than what one does, it is one's basic attitude about the doing which determines what is natural and what is not. If the attitude in planting and nurturing a flower is such that one *feels* participation in the natural flow of things, then one does not add to the delusion of separateness. But if one truly feels that he or she is actually *doing* the growing of the plant, even if one never touches it, a sense of separation will occur. Many of us who love to have plants around, who enjoy being with the green things, still use phrases like, "I am growing tulips in the front yard." There is no harm meant in this, but the words do reflect that subtle separation-sense which creeps in repeatedly, reflecting that one is more a manager than a participant.

Children are growing "things" too, and parents are, so to speak, the gardeners. What is our attitude toward the growth of our children? We cannot deny that again and again we feel that we are growing them at best, building them at worst. "I tried to raise my children the best way I could." I tried to raise. As was the case with plants, this attitude is bound to make objects of the children, and to keep us separate from them.

It is quite possible to move into an attitude of participation in growth, but such a transformation requires something which feels like sacrifice. One of course would sacrifice the feeling of being in control of things. There is some threat in this, but it really doesn't go too deep. A careful, honest scrutiny of the situation reveals that one really isn't very much in control of things anyway. So all that is sacrificed here is a wistful delusion.

Perhaps a greater sacrifice is that one cannot take credit for the growing. One can marvel, celebrate, enjoy, revere and honor the growing of plants and children, but one cannot take credit for doing it. Awesome, joyful participation is a part of growing. But pride really doesn't have a place.

There is a flip side to this question of pride, which requires an even deeper sacrifice. If one cannot take ultimate credit for the growing process, one also cannot assume ultimate blame if the process "fails" in one way or another. This point is easily misunderstood, but it must remain.

Parents and gardeners generally do the best they can at any given point. If they do their best at participating in growth, credit and blame are meaningless. If the child or the plant should wither in one way or another, there is room for sadness and grief, but not for blame. The only time when personal guilt and blame are justified is when through conscious, malicious, manipulative intent, one has done one's worst instead of one's best. Within the attitude of *doing* the growing or *killing* the growing, there is plenty of room for credit and blame. But in the attitude of participation, both must be sacrificed.

There is no doubt that this is a very real sacrifice. Feeling somehow as if one *must* be motivated by desire for credit or fear of blame, what is to be expected if one were suddenly to be liberated from both? The spaciousness of this possibility is awesome.

Perception of true growth means to realize that one is not doing the growth. To fully recognize that the parent is not inside the child, causing cells to multiply, blood to circulate or vitamins to be digested. To perceive that neither parent nor child is doing that. But that it is simply, wonderfully happening.

In delusion, the verb "to grow" is transitive. It has a subject and an object. "I grow you." In sanity, "to grow" is intransitive. One can only say "You are growing." But perhaps even this is inaccurate. Perhaps "growing" is really almost a noun. "Growing is happening."

HEALING

All that has been said of growing can be said of healing. Too often one thinks of the physician or psychotherapist as "one who heals," but *nobody ever heals anybody else*. No one person ever heals another. Nor does any one person heal himself or herself. Like growth, healing is a natural process, as much as ongoing part of us as the beating of our hearts.

If you cut your skin, you bleed for a while, and then the blood clots. *Who* or *what does* that? A scab forms and if you don't pick at it too much, the cells of your skin multiply, rejoining, covering the broken spot. Who or what does that? At this level, the healing process is almost identical to the growth process; a multiplication and refinement of cells and function. It happens. You don't do it; at least not with any will. And most decidedly the doctor does not do it. As with growth, one can only say "Healing is happening." No subject. No object.

This is true for all healing, whether physical or psychological. If I have a bad cut, the doctor will bring the skin edges together with stitches. Hopefully the doctor will do his or her best, and I will be grateful. But this is not healing. Any more than sprinkling fertilizer on plants or giving vitamins to children is growing. What the doctor does is bring the skin back into a more natural state, line it up, cleanse it and put on a bandage; all so that healing *can occur* with a minimum of pain and disfigurement. If I break a bone, the doctor will set it straight and put it in a cast. But this is not healing. It is helping healing, hopefully participating in healing, but it *is* not healing. It is making things more natural and giving the bone a rest so that the healing process can occur more fully.

Whatever the illness or injury, the role of the physician is relegated to three primary activities:

1. To bring the diseased or injured part back into a more natural state.
2. To cleanse and purify.
3. To provide rest.

All that these procedures do is make the setting more convenient for the natural healing process to take place. With infections, the role of antibiotics is to purify and cleanse. The same is true of surgery for appendicitis.

Without the physician, sometimes healing will not occur. Sometimes the injury or illness is too great, and death happens whether or not the physician is present. But sometimes the presence of the physician makes the difference between life and death. Even so, this does not mean that the physician does the healing. The physician simply plays a part, just as my white blood cells play a part in fighting infection. Sometimes the part of the physician is necessary to the healing process. But without the rest of the healing process, the physician could do nothing but autopsies.

It is not too difficult to realize the natural healing process when one is talking about the body. But sometimes the natural healing process is more difficult to see functioning in the human mind. Yet every psychotherapist has seen it, time and time again. When psychotherapy *is* helpful in terms of a specific psychological problem, it is because therapy has presented a clearer vision of reality, which constitutes "a bringing of the diseased part into a more natural state." And because therapy has seen the eradication of irrational fears, obsessions and worries, which amounts to *purification and cleansing*. And it has encouraged self-acceptance and minimized anxiety, thus *giving rest*. But these factors alone mean nothing. There is something else that happens in a troubled mind. Something which results in integration, renewed functioning, and a wholesome, meaningful approach to life. That something has not been "done" by either therapist or client. That something is healing.

Just as there is a need for someone to plough the field or plant the seed or parent the child or suture the cut, there is often a need for someone to participate in the healing process of the mind. Someone to help foster the conditions of naturalness, cleanliness and rest, so that healing can occur more fully. But in the same regard, just as alienation is compounded by the gardener's feeling that he or she is doing the growing, or the parent the raising, or the physician the healing, it perpetuates insanity to feel that either psychotherapist or client is doing the healing of the mind. And it is blatant insanity to feel that either is *fixing* the mind.

There is nothing radical about this idea. Physicians and psychotherapists, off duty and over cocktails, would be the first to admit that all they really do is plough the ground for healing. But in the office, or in the operating room, or in the psychiatric ward, it all seems to change. Then, in the midst of all the *doing*, both therapist and "patient" dive back into the delusion that one is to be fixed and the other is the fixer. All too often. They go crazy together.

The dichotomy between an attitude of participation in healing and an attitude of *doing* the healing occurs everywhere. It is not confined to the doctor's office. One can see it clearly in the way one approaches one's own mind. If some psychological problem occurs, some fear or ambivalence or worry, one naturally does one's best with it. Usually this involves some attempt to bring things back to normal, to cleanse, and to rest. But often people don't stop at that. They don't allow the natural healing to occur. They keep picking at the emotional scab, rewrapping the psychological bandage, reopening the mental wound. Checking to see if it's doing all right. Applying this technique or that method. Picking at it again and again. All the time feeling that they are trying to heal themselves.

With this kind of picking at one's mind, healing may find it difficult to happen. The attempts to make things more natural wind up making things more contrived and artificial. The attempts to cleanse wind up adding more and more contaminants. And the attempts to give rest wind up making greater and greater demands. I laugh at myself in this repeatedly. "Don't bother me," I say to my family. "I've had a rough day and I'm trying to rest." Trying very hard to rest. Working at it, even.

But if one simply did one's best, did what one could do to respond to a problem, and then allowed room for healing— gave space and light and air for healing to happen—that's when healing *can* happen. When it's allowed. This seems to require an element of trust. That with one's fingers *out* of the wound, resting instead of meddling, healing just might happen. Or it requires despair. Realizing that no amount of additional meddling will make the healing any better anyway, so that one might as well rest. Either trust or despair is necessary. And either one will permit the healing to happen.

9

THE LESSONS
OF
SANITY

And starting fresh as from a second birth,
Man in the sunshine of the world's new spring
Shall walk transparant like some holy thing!

Thomas Moore

If the delusion of separation and thingness and fixing dies, and
if sanity is finally allowed to be free, what will sanity tell us
about growing and healing and living?

Being far from sane myself, it is presumptuous of me to
predict. But like most psychotherapists, I do have something to
say about it.

It would be better to attend to the words of those who are
truly sane. Those whose being prompted the great religions of
the world, for example, have clearly spoken a truth that rever-
berates in thousands of hearts. But of course they have also
been misunderstood.

In the midst of delusion, it is difficult to discern the
whereabouts of those who speak the truth. And once found, it
is hard to know whether we understand them. To whom
should one listen? And in what ways should one try to understand?

Knowing all too well the inadequacy of intellect in "figuring out" the truth, perhaps it would be best to listen with

the heart as well as with the mind. To trust, or at least begin to trust, that what is true will resonate with the unborn sanity within us and that what is false will not. In the last analysis, one has no other test of truth anyway. There really is no other choice.

It is in this way that I have compiled the material which follows. Listening to teachers and looking into quietness, these ideas have resonated with me. Keeping in mind that I claim no special authority here, it would be well for you to ask your own intuition about these ideas. If they fail to "connect" with you, let them pass. If they do resonate with your own deep sense of truth, simply listen to the harmony. They imply no special action. *Nothing needs to be done about them.*

I. *ATTITUDE TOWARD MIND*

People characteristically think of mind as a thing. Or in more sophisticated terms, a process. Sanity of course does not see mind as a thing. But it goes on to ask if mind is a process, who is having that process and what is being processed? Perhaps the mind is like the seasons of the year, changing, having impact, but never to be caught or frozen into something solid. One can experience autumn, be in the midst of it, sense it. But one can not hold it; not without robbing it of its life. Mind is the same way. It is not possible to catch a thought and hold it.

So mind cannot fully be understood by objective analysis. One cannot deduce the basic function of mind or describe "its" nature. Mind cannot be figured out. But this does not mean one cannot know and understand mind fully and deeply. It is possible to see mind happening, closely, immediately. Thoughts can be seen arising in consciousness, taking form and passing on. Emotions can be seen erupting like sudden rainstorms, building with great energy and ending in absolute stillness. But this way of knowing mind is not deductive or analytical. It is very intimate and direct. One can learn something *about* a rainstorm by studying meteorology. But to fully know, one must feel the rain upon one's face.

When we *do* learn something about the mind, we always want to *use* that learning. To put the knowledge to good use. As if value lay only in use. Who is it that wants to use this knowledge, and for what ends? Perhaps knowledge is like fertilizer, heaped about the roots of a tree. Must one then try to push the fertilizer into the roots? Pull it up through the cells of the trunk? Drive it into the leaves and instruct it to turn green?

Sometimes it is obvious that the agony within one's mind is caused by one's own hands. That suffering and complexity are created by the presence of one's own fingers, pulling and pushing, directing and redirecting, picking and manipulating. Even realizing this, one tends to think that *more* such activity will bring peace. It is helpful to remember that hands can stroke gently in order to appreciate texture. And that they can spread wide in awe. And that they can fold quietly in reverence. Or open in love.

You probably wish to love your mind. You can, but remember that loving something does not mean making it the way you want it to be. Remember that loving something means allowing it to fully, freely be exactly what it is.

You also probably wish to trust your mind. You can, if you would give it a chance to be trusted. Resting for a moment in one's attempts to *make* the mind trustworthy, one will see the mind *becoming* trustworthy. This need not be accepted on faith. To so do would require that one kill one's fears, and that of course would be simply more manipulation. But slowly, if the mind is given a chance now and then, quietly, you may *discover* that it can be trusted.

Rather than learning how to make mind trustworthy, perhaps we need to learn how to leave our minds alone. For it is only then that we will discover how reliable they truly are.

II. *CONSCIOUSNESS*

Most people, most of the time, are concerned with the *contents* of consciousness. Perhaps it is more valuable to watch consciousness itself. Preoccupied with the sounds one hears, perhaps one misses the silence from which they come. Watching clouds, does one neglect the sky?

We tend to feel consciousness is a creation of the brain, but where is it when one sleeps or dreams? And we tend to feel that consciousness is our possession. Sanity asks us to consider, at least for a moment, that we may be the possessions of consciousness.

There is a habitual assumption that one must do something about every thing that enters consciousness. That one must somehow manage it all. And this takes tremendous energy, causing us to block many things out of awareness so that a few things can be managed well. Sanity asks why this must be so. Why does one feel one must judge every stimulus, evaluate each sensation, respond with desire or fear to every idea, or at barest minimum, label what one sees? To be able to do these things is wonderful. But to *have* to do them is slavery.

Everyone has experienced the indescribable beauty of clearly seeing a flower and never once calling it "flower." Sanity simply asks that this be remembered.

III. *PAYING ATTENTION*

Having to label, judge and respond to everything which enters consciousness, one comes to feel one can be aware of only a few things at once. What do we do with the rest? We shut out millions upon millions of stimuli, saving only those which seem "important." We erect barriers against perception, barriers that take a lot of work to keep up.

The barrier against internal stimuli is called "repression." The barrier against external stimuli is called "paying attention." Paying attention means to block out many things so that one or two can be dealt with. But paying attention makes nothing more clear. It simply shuts out what one feels is "irrelevant." Paying attention is what keeps you from hearing that sound in the background, and from feeling the book in your hands as you read. Paying attention takes much effort, and one becomes tired afterwards.

Sanity questions whether paying attention to something is always necessary. It hints that it is possible to relax the barriers against perception, allowing countless things to come fully into awareness, and not have to pay attention to any one. And that it is also possible to be acutely aware of one thing without shutting anything else out. And even that it is possible to pay absolute attention to nothing at all. Whether one *should* do this or not is something which can be learned from experience and exploration. But that one *can* do it is something one should know.

IV. BEING AWARE

Immediate awareness is a gift, the purpose of which is to see living. But most of the time we want awareness to be a tool. Becoming immediately aware of living, we *use* that awareness to evaluate the living. To think *about* living. And as soon as this happens, awareness is gone again. Kidnapped. Immediate awareness has assumed the quality of a judging parent, asking "Should I be doing this?" or "How well am I doing this?" and in the process awareness becomes uncomfortable.

So, much of the time, one goes about living unaware. Eyes blinded to the wonder of the immediate moment, consciousness glued to a task or lost in fantasy. As if one feels it is more comfortable to be a robot than a harassed little child.

Sanity proclaims that immediate awareness is simply a state of appreciation. One need do *nothing, nothing at all* with it. It is a gift, freely given. Immediate awareness is the clear clean air without which healing and growth are stunted. The question is whether one can receive this gift as freely and gently as it is given. Whether one can allow space for one's being to breathe.

V. *DESIRE*

Most of the time we assume we are motivated by desire. That without being driven by desire or repulsion we would cease to act. And so we hold desire and fear, clinging to them as if they were our very source of energy. But perhaps one would not stagnate without them. Perhaps motivation could come from beyond them. From the simple situation at hand.

You are standing on a corner with your child. He steps into the street and you quickly pull him back. Must it be said that you did this because you desired to keep him alive, or because you feared for his safety? Is it not possible that you pulled him back because he stepped into the street?

Consider that desire and fear might simply be the salt and pepper of life. Serving to help you savor your being. That rather than determining behavior, they simply give it color and interest.

One may try to overcome desire. And yet one knows that

fighting desire makes it stronger than before. Waging war against it makes it an enemy. Is it not possible for there to be space between desire and behavior, killing neither, appreciating both?

VI. *NEUROSIS*

One assumes that neurosis is a defective way of living. Inexorable habits, insurmountable fears, undying thoughts and feelings. A burden weighing down the shoulders of one's life. And so we struggle with the pieces of neurosis. Experiencing a neurotic fear, one tries to work it through, understand it, express it, suppress it, counteract it or bypass it. All of which are designed to get rid of it.

But everything one does to get rid of neurosis makes it seem more real. More important. More like something to be rid of. And if a piece of it is destroyed, something else inevitably comes to take its place.

Perhaps one must recognize that there is no way out. It is possible to adjust neurosis, restructure it, make it more socially acceptable and temporarily more comfortable, but there is no way out. For in trying to get out, one continues to make credible that from which one is fleeing. It cannot be done. In one blink of the eyes another reality can be seen, the freely being immediate present, where neither self nor neurosis continues to be defined, but one cannot "get there."

But perhaps healing could be allowed. Treating your self with gentleness, accepting fully, seeing clearly, being fully as you are, *being* as neurotic as you are, healing might happen. Healing occurs when awareness is open and when acceptance is total. But the acceptance must be so complete that it even includes love for all one's attempts to fix one's self.

VII. *PSYCHOSIS*

There is an assumption that psychosis comes when one goes beyond one's self. That the worst insanity arises when ego crumbles and dissolves. And therefore we tend to uphold the worth of ego strength, fortifying and bolstering it until self determines all.

But consider that psychosis may be the result of struggling to *regain* ego. That the symptoms of insanity are the clutching fingers of a mind trying to regain control, unwilling or unable to give up.

If one becomes psychotic, perhaps it is because one has touched the face of God and could not relinquish the importance of self. Considering this, one cannot help but find compassion.

VIII. *ACCEPTANCE*

Always there is a desire to accept some things and reject others. Who is making this choice, and with what wisdom? Does one accept what feels good and reject what does not? And where does the acceptance come from? Figuring out the strategies of acceptance, one walks into a jungle in which the paths branch and branch until irrevocable blindness is finally realized.

Acceptance of this or of that is jungle exploration, and beautiful as such. But as a way out of the jungle it does not work. If you feel *you* must choose to accept or not to accept, then realize that you might choose to accept *everything*. Total, complete acceptance is a very real possibility. It involves accepting beauty and ugliness. And accepting responsibility and laziness, both, completely. It even means accepting one's own inability to accept.

Perhaps this sounds like nothing. Like nothing happening at all. But in accepting everything, one cannot help but let one's self be. What is the quality of *this* kind of nothing?

IX. RESPONSIBILITY

Behavior needs to be responsible. But who is responsible *for* that behavior? If *you* choose between this and that, then *you* are responsible. To conceive that there may be no substantial "you" behind behavior is no excuse for avoiding responsibility. For conception and realization are not the same. As long as one still believes in one's sense of self, one is responsible.

It is only when self-importance truly ceases that all behavior springs with inherent responsibility from the situation at hand, and yet there is no one there being responsible. This may be absolutely true, but it is at the same time a pipe dream. Can two realities be perceived at once? Perhaps it is not so important, because the fact is that as long as one *does* feel responsible, one is.

Thus it is possible to affirm responsibility, and even self-determination. But remember that responsibility is the road which travels between guilt and pride. And that guilt and pride both serve the sense of self. Remember that responsibility is the bridge between credit and blame. Which are also servants of one's image of one's self.

To strive for pride and credit at the expense of guilt and blame is both human and delightful. But to rail against the pain one feels in this struggle is but a temper tantrum. Pride cannot be without guilt, nor credit without blame. Just as happiness cannot be without sadness. Biting into the completeness of this life, appreciating its flavor, one can live richly. But always both sides must be tasted equally.

And if one side is sacrificed, so must the other be. To go

beyond the polarities of responsibility, all must be affirmed equally, or all must be denied equally. Transcendence does not play favorites. Neither is transcendence something which can be done, for any attempt to *do* transcendence must come from desire for happiness or for release from pain. Recognizing this, it is possible to rest *in* responsibility, not *from* it.

X. *LOVE*

We think of loving someone. As if love were something one could create, give or receive. Often we even feel that love is something one "should" do. And then one may begin to wonder if one is capable of loving.

Who does the loving? Consider that loving cannot be "done" by anyone. When love is recognized, it is already there. Happening. It can be discovered, its presence can be recognized, but it can never be manufactured. And though love may be buried from awareness, it cannot be killed. So there really is no question as to whether one is capable of loving. The only question is whether one is capable of seeing the love which is already there.

We tend to think of love as attachment, binding, bonding and committing. But love is only free. Love accepts and allows totally. Because there is oneness in love, there is no giving and no taking. There is not even relationship. What does it really mean to *be in* love? Not that I have love for you, but that you and I are *in* love? We exist, as one, immersed in love, more deeply than in the air we breathe.

And this "self" which creeps in upon freely being time and time again. Can it be loved? It certainly need not be hated. Only love will free it to be what it will be, while hatred can but force it into more and more rigid, frozen postures. Discover then, the love that is there for your self and for your predicament.

Searching beneath anxiety, one will find fear. And beneath fear hurt will be discovered. Beneath the hurt will be guilt. Beneath the guilt lie rage and hatred. But do not stop with this, for beneath the rage lies frustrated desire. Finally, beneath and beyond desire, is love. In every feeling, look deeply. Explore without ceasing. At bottom, love is. Realizing this, need one do anything about the anxiety one feels?

XI. WORK

Work is generally thought of as pushing against something. Overcoming a resistance. Force. And we assume that something not requiring work is of little value. But where is the work of being alive? Does life have greater value if one works at living? Or does perhaps work have value because one *is* living?

Perhaps true work involves overcoming no resistances, but rather learning to relax in such a way that no resistances exist. Lifting a brick to build a wall, you see your hand moving the brick. But in one blink of the eyes, you can see hand and brick moving together.

The difference between work and play is only a matter of attitude. Work, fully done, is play. When the body works, it is dancing. When the mind works, it is dreaming. Appreciating the joys and sadnesses of both, one moves within the process of life.

XII. SUFFERING

One nearly always seeks to avoid pain. And one nearly always struggles with pain when it comes. Must one manage one's self away from pain? If your hand touches a flame, must *you* pull it away? Or does your hand simply pull away, because of the pain?

It is helpful to look at the difference between pain and suffering. Pain is a stimulus, like cold or green. There will be a response. But suffering is you or I struggling against our pain. Pain can exist freely, without suffering, as when you pinch your skin or stretch very hard before relaxing.

Suffering is the effort one puts against one's pain, beyond response, beyond healing. Suffering is what one heaps on top of pain, the second-guessing of pain, the raging against what is, the refusal to accept what is happening.

Consider that one can allow one's pain to be cared for, through one's own natural responses, without any special management. Then where there was suffering is only space.

XIII. *LIVING*

We feel we have life right now, but really life has us for this moment. Therefore there is no need to try to live. Even in the extremities of crisis, there is no need for any special attempt to live. For living, in and of itself, will struggle to go on.

One can choose to live or die, but again one must ask who does the choosing. One can choose this again and again, and perhaps this could make one feel powerful. But the role of choice in life most deeply is simply to determine whether one will be *aware* of living or not. Whether one goes through the motions of living like a sleepwalker, or whether one awakens to the process now. Too often in searching for a richer life, a fuller life, one's eyes become blinded to the immediate wonder of the life that is. Sometimes we pray, "If I should die before I wake . . ." But perhaps a deeper prayer would be "If I should wake before I die . . ."

If one can discover love for one's search for a better

life, without attempting to destroy it, and if one can find compassion for the striving, then the beauty of this very moment will not be missed.

We often feel that "To be or not to be" is the question.

"To be or to try to be," that is more the question.

10

FREELY
BEING
RESPONSIBLE

I am the captain of my soul;
I rule it with stern joy;
And yet I think I had more fun
When I was a cabin boy.

Keith Preston, *An Awful Responsibility*

Sanity, at least as I have pictured it, seems to be telling us to allow ourselves to be what we are, fully, dynamically and without any great extra meddling. To simply, freely be. It is saying that peace and fullness lie in giving up the struggle to master one's self.

This is a very tantalizing possibility. But it is also easily misunderstood and abused. Words like acceptance, allowing, giving up and letting be can encourage passivity and irresponsibility. Sometimes it seems very difficult to walk the line between arrogant self-responsibility and passive lethargy. I think the answer is to be found by stepping into a different dimension of self-perception. Getting back away from the laziness-arrogance polarity and seeing more of the totality of any given situation. Then, moving *into* the situation, what needs to be done will become clear. And the complexities of figuring out what is responsible and what is not become irrelevant. One winds up simply doing what needs to be done.

It may be of help to look at the story of one man's struggle with responsibility and freely being. This man happens to have been a drug addict. If this should make it a bit difficult for you to identify with him, it might be valuable for you to consider your own addictions. Everyone has addictions. Any "bad" habit which we find ourselves wanting to "overcome" is an addiction. Whether it is to drugs, alcohol, food, tobacco, sex, television, sports, self-importance, power or work, the basic quality is the same. One does something because it makes one feel good now. Later on there may be a price to pay, but now it feels good. And the more we do it, the more desire there is to do it again. As with popcorn or potato chips, it's hard to stop at just one. An understanding of one's own addictions makes it a bit easier to understand those of people who are labeled as "junkies" or "alcoholics."

When I first met John he was twenty-three years old and addicted to heroin. He was short, skinny and pale, but his eyes were deep and lively. He came to the clinic for "help" with his drug problem, but his motivation was not the most pure. Like many other clients of the clinic he came under duress. He'd been apprehended in an attempt to steal money from the office of the construction company where he worked, and the court had given him the choice of getting help or going to jail.

In our first interview it was obvious that John was intelligent, but his intelligence had been of little help to him. Coming from a lower-middle-class family, with alcoholic parents who separated when he was very young, he had never quite been able to find a direction in life. It had seemed to him that his school teachers, his bosses on the job, and the public authorities were all harassing him rather than helping, and he had essentially given up on life. At least that's the way he described it.

"Every time I'd get some idea about doing something constructive with my life, I'd get shot down. I wanted to be a musician, but the school didn't have music lessons. I tried to write, but the teachers always gave me Ds and Fs because of my bad grammar. They never saw what I was trying to say. There was nobody at home I could talk to—Mom was always tired trying to take care of us five kids. So anyway, I started smoking some dope with friends and it made me feel O.K. You know . . . like there wasn't anything to worry about. Then I just started doing harder drugs. I still want to make something of myself, but now I'm addicted and I gotta get some help."

Most psychotherapists would see, from these few words, that John is immature, that he has some problems with authority figures, and that he tends to blame others for his problems rather than taking responsibility for himself. Also that he's probably more interested in getting out of trouble than in really bettering himself. All these insights would be essentially true, but there's another dimension which has to be investigated. I asked John how he felt about himself as a person in this world, what he thought about the meaning of life.

"It's a crummy world, and there's no sense fighting it. I just gotta get along the best I can. If I could get some real big money, like those dudes in Washington [politicians] I'd be as good as anybody. But they keep you down. I'm as good as the next guy, but I never had a chance."

I asked about any religious feelings he had.

"I used to go to church with my mother. She used to make us go. I couldn't stand it. All them hypocrites acting holier-than-thou, and then going out and knifing people in the back to get money. They talk about love and they run around on their wives. They look down on junkies like me while they're drinking their martinis. It makes me want to barf."

At the beginning of the interview John had been passive, uninvolved, apathetic. But now he was showing some steam. He really seemed angry. I asked him about God.

"You're gonna think this is crazy, but LSD is God. God's

supposed to make you feel all right in this world. He's supposed to love you, right? Well the only time I feel at home in this world is when I'm tripping on acid. That's God. And don't try to lay anything on me about getting high on God without drugs. I've heard that before and it's a lot of bull. Those Jesus freaks are worse than junkies. They're cop-outs just as much as drugs. Only they think they're better than anyone else."

"What are they copping out from?" I asked.

"You know, when they want something they sit around and pray for it. Me, I go out and get it. And when they got problems they smile and say, 'God will take care of it.' Me, I shoot up some good heroin and any problems I got are taken care of."

"Until you come down."

"Right. But they're no better'n me. They live in a fantasy world. I live in a drug world. It's no different. They take their hassles to God. I take mine to dope. We're all copping out."

"What wouldn't be a cop-out?"

"To go right in and handle the problems you got. Get busy and do something about 'em. Get a job, get married, raise a family, do your thing. That's why I wanna get off this dope. I want to get straight, make some money and start a life for myself. I'm sick and tired of copping out."

Thus far, John's feelings have been about the same as thousands of other drug-addicted persons who walk into clinics for help. And the course he followed for the next couple of months was also typical. There was an attempt to kick the narcotic habit, but he couldn't do it. He was drug free for several days, but then he got into an argument with his boss and walked off the job, bought some heroin and started "shooting up" again.

"I couldn't make it. You can't kick dope this way. I want to get on the methadone program."

At first, John blamed his getting back on drugs to the severity of his craving. But when I pressed him about it he said he really felt O.K. without the drugs, until he got into the fight with his boss. Then he started feeling an old feeling.

"It's like you can't win. Every time things start to go right there's someone around to hassle you. My boss wouldn't trust me with the keys to the office. He said he was afraid I'd steal something. He said I should be grateful that he took me back on the job at all, after I stole from him the first time. I guess I can understand his not trusting me, but how you going to get anywhere if nobody gives you a chance? Man, I still want to get out there and do good, but it seems like there's no hope."

John went into a second phase of his "treatment." He took the drug methadone which stopped his physical craving for dope, and the therapy that went along with the methadone was geared toward helping him realize that he was responsible for himself. He agreed that he was responsible for himself. He said he knew that all along. And he'd show everyone how responsible he was if he were just given the chance.

The "chance" came when he got a promotion on the job after several months of good work. He said he was making enough money to get married. He'd already bought a car and had enough for a deposit on an apartment. He was very bright and hopeful. The entire clinic celebrated his marriage. His wife was very young but very much in love with him. Two weeks later she ran off with another man.

John immediately left his job, left the clinic, and went back to street drugs. He was admitted to the hospital a few weeks later after an overdose of heroin.

"O.K., you don't have to tell me," he said, "I did it myself. I should have handled it differently. I'm responsible for getting back on drugs. I'm just too weak. I copped out again."

After John got out of the hospital and back into the clinic program, we started talking more about his sense of responsibility. It rapidly became clear that though his behavior and words were often irresponsible, he had always felt *very* responsible. *I* want this and *I'm* going to get it. Those guys are always hassling me so *I'm* going to quit trying. Even in blaming others for his own failures, he still felt responsible *for letting "them" win.* He felt weak and impotent, and to feel weak and impotent is to feel very responsible. He told me of a fantasy which occurred in various forms: in dreams, daydreams, and under LSD.

"I'm walking down this city street and I'm very small. About the size of a pea. All the people are huge. The buildings are mammoth. I'm scared by my smallness. Weak. Helpless. But I have this magic phrase I say. 'Snow go, snow go, snow go.' And then it starts to snow, and as it snows on me I get bigger and bigger, like a giant snowman, and everybody gets scared of me."

In street jargon, heroin is often called "snow." But the importance of this fantasy is deeper than the idea that heroin compensates for feelings of inferiority. The important thing is that he wants to be big and powerful, and he *does* something to make this happen. He wants to loom over other people rather than have them loom over him, and he *makes* it happen. He chants his magic words and it begins to snow and he gets big. The important thing is that he did it. He's responsible for it.

At another time he described his feelings when he'd insert a needle into a vein to inject heroin. He really liked doing that. "I don't know why, it just feels good." He, like many other people addicted to narcotics, said, "I could get high off of just shooting up, even if it were water." The good feeling here is that *he is doing something to himself* which will have a powerful impact. A sense of effectiveness upon himself. A sense of responsibility. *I* did it. *I'm* effective.

In a distorted way, John was a very responsible person. A real self-determiner. He felt very badly about himself and often got depressed when things didn't go well, but he never wanted to let go of his sense of responsibility.

In this light it can be seen that in blaming others for his own faults, John was really trying to hold on to a sense of responsibility. To admit that he had failed, through his own fault only, would mean that he was a nobody. That he was incapable of responsibility. But in blaming others he could say, "I'm responsible for my actions. I want to do right. They're just too big and powerful for me. They beat me every time."

A lot of rage goes with this. Anger against himself for being weak, and anger against others for being strong. So his reaction was usually to do something he could see as assertive and responsible. Destructive, but still assertive and responsible. Like walking off the job. "I ain't going to let them treat me that way." Or stealing from "them." Or shooting dope.

Irresponsibility in our society is usually taken to mean a free-wheeling, do-what-feels-good, thoughtless, motiveless attitude. This is just a superficial interpretation. What looks like irresponsibility is usually very powerful. There are usually heavy, grinding motives. John, for example, was at war. He was waging battle after battle to protect his own sense of power and responsibility.

John described this process in some detail when he discussed getting fired from his job.

"I went to work that day with the best of intentions. No drugs for several days. I was going to do a good job and I even thought I might ask the boss for a raise that day or the next. I was supposed to get some papers from the office, and that's when he said he couldn't trust me with the keys."

I asked him what he felt, immediately, right then.

"Shocked. Then that changed to anger. Ah, in between the shock and anger I guess I was hurt. He didn't trust me to be responsible. Yeah, and then I thought 'Well he doesn't have any reason to trust me—I did try to rob him.' But there wasn't anything I could do about that. *That's* what really made me angry. I was feeling angry with him, but I was really angry because there wasn't anything I could *do*. So I walked off the job. Like *that* was something I could do. Keep my pride. But when I got home I was so depressed about losing my temper and losing the job, I felt powerless again. So that's when I shot up."

In this sequence John never once let go of seeing himself as responsible. As the determiner of himself. Is it possible that John's problem is too much sense of responsibility rather than not enough? Or is it just that his sense of responsibility is different from the rest of society's?

This question can be carried further by looking at what happened to John as he began to overcome his addiction. The first step was to finally admit that the drug was more powerful than he. That his habit was irrevocably beyond his control. That there was no way he really could be responsible for it. Not that anyone else was responsible. Just that he was powerless to do anything about it himself. This didn't happen until he'd been addicted for many years, and had tried to quit many times. Until he'd struggled in every way he knew and had no choice but to give up. At this point his pattern changed. Always before when he'd given up, he'd done so with anger and willfulness. "To hell with it," he'd say, and turn to something else, equally destructive.

But at this time of giving up, he couldn't be angry anymore. He couldn't have any real feeling, for there was nothing else to turn to and nothing to be angry with. All he could do was give up and live. This was a kind of ultimate admission of *irresponsibility*. "I can't do it." With this, he started to heal. Alcoholics Anonymous knows how important this admission of powerlessness is if healing is to happen, but John had to find out for himself. He also discovered another basic tenet of AA's philosophy; take it a day at a time. John just naturally started living his life one day at a time, because there wasn't any other way to do it. He didn't really fight his urges to use dope. He simply didn't shoot up. He didn't *overcome* the urges. He just didn't respond to them in any way.

Then there came a time when he started to think again. "I've been off drugs for several months now." And there was a bit of pride in his voice. His hunger for responsibility had reoccurred. "I did it. I kicked the habit!" And he began to get excited. Dreams of powerful self-determination arose again. And with the hunger for responsibility came a renewed hunger for heroin. The two had gone together for him for so long that when one returned, the other did too. And with a mind-trick so subtle that only addicts can appreciate it, he said, "I can handle it now. I'll prove it to myself by shooting up just once." And he was off again, off and running and addicted.

The treacherous thing about responsibility is that it so easily becomes hooked to pride, power and self-importance. As long as it is *behavior* which needs to be responsible there is no problem. One does what one needs to do. What is right, appropriate and good. But when responsibility gets hooked to saying powerfully, "*I* can do this. *I* can control my behavior. *I* am responsible," then treachery is close.

Responsible *behavior* and enterprising *action* are necessary, dynamic and beautiful. Responsible behavior and enterprising action are generated by the situation at hand. They spring from all the factors combined in the present situation. From what needs to be done. From the individual's sense of right and wrong. From desires and hopes, impulses and values. All these things go to produce responsible behavior and enterprising action.

But too often, in the individual's internal mental world, responsible behavior and enterprising action are clouded under the thought "I am being responsible," or "I am enterprising." Then what becomes important is not the need of the situation but the significance and power of the "I AM." Then responsibility becomes a useless adornment. An energy-sapping accoutrement which serves only to clutter the situation.

There is one more significant chapter in John's story. After his "slip," he did encounter another time of giving up. This time he was more savvy to the treachery of his sense of responsibility. Or at least he thought so. He recognized that giving up meant giving up. And that there was no room for personal power in any true healing process that might occur in him. So he became quite comfortable with letting himself be.

At first, his letting himself be was very gentle and helpful. It was a natural part of giving up. It meant to accept himself totally, as he found himself at any given time. He described it one day like this:

"I was sitting on the bus, riding to work. All of a sudden I had this surge of laziness. Like 'I don't want to go to work today. I'd rather sleep.' In the past I would have struggled with that—trying to put the feeling out of my mind. And I would have failed, probably. And the struggle would have created more struggles and pretty soon I would have been all knotted up about it. Probably would have taken some dope. But this time I just said to myself, 'O.K., you got a lazy feeling. That's O.K. And you're here on the bus riding to work and that's O.K. too.' And then the impulse wasn't there anymore."

So he'd begun to learn to accept himself and let himself be, and he was doing fine. He was growing into a rewarding, peaceful, dynamic life. But his acceptance wasn't really total, and it began to get him in trouble.

"I'd gone to this party and I was having a good time. There was a girl that I really liked and we hit it off real well. Then somebody started passing around some marijuana. I really wanted to smoke some but I knew it might get me back into the drug scene. So I held off. I realized I was struggling with whether or not to smoke it so I real quick got into letting

myself be. I said to myself, 'You really want to have a smoke
and you're fighting yourself, so relax and do what comes naturally.' I relaxed, and what came naturally was to have a
smoke. Now I've been smoking more. No hard stuff, but it's
got me worried."

The power-responsibility thing came in again here when
he told himself to stop struggling. But what really got him in
trouble was that he couldn't accept himself totally. He thought
he was letting himself fully be, but he'd really been very selec-
tive. When he tuned in to his feelings he was struggling with
himself. There were two armies at war in him. One was saying
"I want a smoke." The other was saying "It'll get you in trouble." If he'd *really* let himself be, he would have accepted
both sides. Just as he had on the bus. He would have accepted
the struggle. But instead, he took sides.

He didn't want to be struggling so he stifled that part of
himself. He didn't want to be manipulating so he said, "I'll do
what comes naturally." In retrospect, this was clearly another
mind-trick. Doing what comes naturally really meant going
ahead and smoking. So he'd stifled his conscience. In attempting to let himself be, he'd rather skillfully managed to get what
his impulses wanted. This is a very subtle but very common
abuse of self-acceptance and of letting one's self be. It so easily
becomes a cop-out. A way of avoiding a necessary struggle.

If John had to think all this through every time a decision
was to be made, he'd be almost paralyzed by the subtleties and
complexities of it all. But eventually he found that the way was
indeed very simple.

"When I've got to make a decision, I don't have to do
anything special. Or *not* do anything special. All I need to do is
accept what's going on in my mind. The only thing is it's got
to be *total* acceptance. If I've got a struggle going on between
an urge and my common sense, I got to accept it *all*, the urge,
my common sense, *and* the struggle. Then it gets worked out

the best way I can. I haven't taken sides or killed anything or added anything. I find I go ahead and do the best I can, and it usually works out fine."

There is wisdom, fear and sacrifice in this way of self-acceptance. The wisdom is in John's realization that he can't really *add* anything of value to his struggle anyway. All he has to work with are his impulses and his common sense, and he might as well let them work it out. By getting involved in the battle in any way other than accepting it, he's only going to cloud the picture and distort the outcome.

The fear is that he's been so used to being responsible *for* himself, he's afraid to let himself *be* responsible. He's afraid it won't work somehow. Hopefully though, the wisdom overshadows the fear and he'll be able to accept and allow himself to be.

The sacrifice is really twofold. The first is a potential sacrifice. If he lets himself work out the conflict between impulse and control, he always runs the risk of not getting what he wants. Or getting what he doesn't want. He may have to do without. If that's the outcome, he'll just have to accept it.

The second sacrifice is that he can't take credit for the outcome. He can't indulge in self-pride or a sense of having "been responsible." His mind and his body worked out the problem within the situation at hand and he can't take credit for it. All he can do is watch. Perhaps he could be permitted some awe, or wonder, or appreciation. Maybe even gratitude for the process which worked through him. But no credit.

All he can do is watch. But the watching is really the important part of it all. Most of the time, especially while he was addicted, John did not watch. His eyes were closed to his being-in-the-present-moment. He went around acting and reacting, waking up only when some strong feeling came along. Some desire or fear or guilt or anger or hope. The rest of the time he was quite unaware of being. And while he was unaware, all sorts of things went on unconsciously. Rage got directed in very destructive ways. Warm, loving impulses got killed. Fear ruled.

But with his eyes open, accepting all, the various forces inside and outside could dance together, freely, dynamically, and the being of John was given space to emerge.

The importance of awareness then is not so that we can better control ourselves. It is not so that we can analyze and interpret our minds or bodies or the world around us. To use awareness as a tool for self-manipulation only leads to treachery. Awareness is a space giver. An open window, letting the fresh air in. It unties the knots and loosens the tension. Awareness with full acceptance is like pure sunlight shining into a cellar, making it possible for healing to happen and growth to take place. One has to do nothing *with* it.

11

GENTLE MEDDLING

Force is no remedy.

John Bright, *On the Irish Troubles*

Sanity speaks clearly when it says, "Be who you are, completely." Recognizing that at core this natural process of being is beyond control, it is tempting to relax totally. But as John found out with his addiction, one cannot fully be if one stifles the desire for change and improvement. So we are left with a dilemma. Sanity lies in just simply being, but for most of us just simply being *includes* some desire to change the way we experience life. The dilemma sounds complex from a rational point of view, but the answer is really quite simple. One simply moves in the direction of accepting one's self more and more completely. Then in the process of this acceptance, sanity simply begins to emerge.

So, recognizing and accepting some continuing need to change, what *does* one *do*? Simply be who you are, completely. Better yet, just realize that you *are* being who you are, right now, completely. That's all.

There are times when that *is* all. When this awareness just happens, easily, naturally. These times are gifts, and all one has to do is accept them, move into them, allow them to be.

But there are many other times when the will to meddle with one's self comes on very strong. Then one cannot "simply" be. One cannot kill one's will to meddle. That must be accepted too. In those times perhaps one *must* meddle with one's self. Then there are perhaps some ways of meddling more gently. Ways which are tender and not severe, open and not grasping, quiet and not noisy. This chapter will present some possibilities for gentle meddling.

But once more let me say that if you can be yourself without feeling that you are meddling, or if you can be relaxed and accepting *of* your meddling, there is no need to do anything extra. The ideas and suggestions in this chapter are for those times when it seems one *must* meddle, and when one cannot even help but meddle with the meddling. These ideas and suggestions are *not* techniques to achieve "just being." They are only touches of gentleness, at best a practice. Perhaps they may ease one's acceptance of just being, but they do not, and never can, produce just being. Just being simply is.

There may occur a tendency to use some of these ways of meddling as escapes from discomfort and difficulty. This warrants close scrutiny, for to escape is to remove or kill a part of one's experience, thus limiting the fullness of life. We all tend to strive for happiness at the expense of sadness; that is naturally human. But to try to *use* freely being to promote one side of life over the other will always be an abuse. So these ideas and suggestions are not ways to bliss without pain. They are simply ways of meddling that one might hope would help clarify one's perception and appreciation of *both* bliss and pain.

At the beginning of Chapter 9 I gave a caution about my own presumptuousness in relating what I felt to be the messages of sanity. This same caution should apply here, along with the major overriding danger flag against using these suggestions as ways of greater rather than less self-manipulation.

I. *GENERAL ATTITUDES*

In all things, above all, be gentle with yourself. Not especially weak, nor especially passive. Just gentle. Nothing should be destroyed, nothing denied, nothing stifled. All goes on, as it will, and hopefully one can be wide awake, deeply within it all.

There should be no detachment or distancing from life, yet there can be a sense of freedom and space within the process of living.

There need be no special activity or passivity. No more or less than is naturally there within you. You are who you are, but there is no need to decide or determine who you are. You do what you do, but there is no need to be actively hooking that doing to an idea of what you ought to do or should do. Such hooking will occur, spontaneously, if allowed. There is no need to manage it. You are who you are no matter what you do, so there is no need to try to be.

II. *SELF-IMAGE*

Forget worrying about who you are. Hold on to no idea of identity. But neither try to destroy any sense of identity that is there. Allow the sense of identity to come and go. No grasping for it. No attack upon it. No clinging to it. No freezing of it.

Evaluate your self only to the point that is natural for you. To the point that feels right and comfortable at the time. Neither add nor subtract anything special. Don't add any extra "I'm proud," or "I'm bad" or "The heck with it" or anything. Simply accept your self-evaluation as it is and then quit.

Whenever and wherever you encounter your self, an image of self, an evaluation of self, a fear for self, a desire for self, self-consciousness, pride or guilt or whatever, don't kill it. There is no need for battle. One needs do nothing special *with* it. Just back off from it a little, see it and take a deep breath. Let it be and its energy will, in time, be free.

Manipulation and fixing of self is like a ladder, each rung building on the one before it. One manipulates, and then manipulates the manipulation. One alters, then alters the alteration. Fixes, and then fixes the fixing. One does need to know when to stop. Without awareness, this can become an endless ladder to despair. But with awareness and humor, the ladder has a final rung. Where rest is possible. So watch your ladder of self-manipulation, and grin.

Let your self be. Totally. Without a single iota of equivocation. Let it all exist, as awful or wonderful as it may seem. Permit it absolutely. If there is a desire to kill something within yourself, ask forthrightly, "Who is killing whom?" And be exceedingly gentle. To struggle with yourself will make you very important.

Self-importance is a trap, but it is not something one can attack directly. If one makes a frontal attack on self-importance, success or failure will foster pride or guilt. And these in turn will make the self even *more* important. So it is foolish to try to stop being interested in one's self. It is much wiser to nurture interest in other "things." In awareness of the immediate present. In whatever work needs to be done. In the sun and the wind. And in other people. It is wise to be with others, in friendship, teamwork and community. For if one can be interested in others, openly, with no cultism or competition, the importance of private-selfhood just might be forgotten for a while. In giving without hope of receiving anything in return, not even the pride of "I am being good," being can become unfettered. Sanity can never be a completely private matter.

III. *LOOSENING AND OPENING*

Search within both mind and body for anything that is tight, and allow it to loosen. Look for anything which is being held and relax that holding, as if you were slowly opening your hands and letting go. Whatever is being held, one can ease one's grip.

In the midst of any situation, no matter how tense or pressing, it is possible to relax. First the body, just easing the muscles and allowing the limbs to become flexible. Then the mind, in the same way, relaxing. Not avoiding the tension of the moment, it is possible to relax *into* it. Deeply.

Wherever one finds oneself managing, stifling, killing, controlling, grasping, holding, craving or struggling, and where one cannot accept these things going on, it is possible to slip their bonds. In any given moment, you can simply step aside from this tightness, as if you were slipping out of an old overcoat and gently walking away. Perhaps in the next moment the tightness will return. But then relaxation can happen again. Permanence is a myth at any rate. One may think about life in terms of days and years. But one may live it only in this very instant.

There are knots, tight places, in every aspect of living. Body, mind, moving, talking, thinking, seeing, eating, loving, everything has its knots. Whenever a knot is found, it can be allowed to loosen and perhaps unravel completely. Never by picking at the knot itself, but rather by easing the tension upon it. It is helpful here to take a deep breath and let it out, allowing the tension to go with it.

IV. *TRUSTING MIND*

Practice trusting your mind. For a few minutes every day, give your mind a chance to be. If you have regular prayer or meditation times, you can do this too. Or you can set aside a special time. Or simply do it whenever it seems right.

1. Sit down, or lie down, and take a few minutes to get physically comfortable.

2. Take a few deep breaths to relax. Brightly waking up as you breathe in, relaxing your body as you breathe out.
3. Relax your face, your shoulders, your stomach, and your breathing.
4. Then, for a few minutes, just be. Allow your mind to do what it wants. Have no expectations for it, ask nothing of it, just let it be. If it wishes to be noisy, let it be noisy. If it wishes to be quiet, let it be quiet. If it wants to go off on a fantasy, O.K. If it wants to be bored or blissful, scared or angry, let it be.
5. For these few minutes, don't try to do anything special. And don't try not to do anything special. Just be.

V. *EXPECTATIONS*

Expectations are the long arm of desire, reaching forward in time and attempting to force reality to produce what one wants. If expectations are satisfied, a sense of power may evolve. If they are not satisfied, one may become disappointed with life. Expectations are bound to happen, but they do not have to be taken too seriously. If expectations are not held too strongly, they will rise and fall of their own accord, adding nothing but color to the process of living. They become accoutrements of life rather than the reasons for living. Underneath, it is possible to move toward an attitude of expecting absolutely nothing. Nothing.

Then one can move into life with openness. It is as if one says to the world, and to life, and to one's self, and to God, "Surprise me!" In marriage for example, this simple shift of attitude can make the difference between boredom and beauty. One awakens in the morning to find one's spouse is still there! The children gather for breakfast! How marvelous!

VI. DESIRES

Once one has discovered that desire is not the primary motivation for living, an entirely new approach to life is possible. In the process it is tempting to want to overcome some of one's desires. This can be very freeing, but it can also become a trap of tenseness. If desire is to be given up, one must also give up the desire to be desireless. So perhaps it is better simply to loosen one's grip on desire. Take it less seriously. See it clearly rather than engage it in a taut battle. Watching any desire closely and immediately, it is often surprising to see that the desire lasts for only a few moments. It may return again soon. But each time its tenure is very brief. There is some release in this. And one experiences a tendency to laugh.

Recognizing this coming and going of desire, it becomes evident that any prolonged wanting comes more from an *idea* of desiring than from the impulse itself. Then it is possible to let go of any idea of wanting, and the entire sphere of desire becomes open, spacious.

If you do decide to limit your pleasure directly, it is wise to do so only to the extent that feels like lightness, openness and freedom. If it becomes heavy and serious, this is a signal that sacrifice is being overdone. And probably one is *wanting* very much to be without desire. Perhaps it is better not to initiate too many extra sacrifices. But when the opportunity for sacrifice comes along, be willing to accept it. This way, one is not so much in the business of choosing and managing one's own sacrifices.

VII. ACCEPTANCE

Things are as they are whether one accepts them or not.

So they may as well be accepted. If one can accept everything, just as it is, totally, one simply can be. But *total* acceptance is very rare. There can be no exceptions if acceptance is total. Nothing withheld. If this kind of acceptance sounds passive, then it is incomplete. One has forgotten to accept one's desire to change things. If one can accept each situation just as it is, and also accept one's own reaction to that situation, just as it is, there is nothing left but wonder.

Acceptance of one's self is often more difficult than acceptance of a situation. But anywhere, any time, it is possible to do the best one can and then say something like, "I accept," or "Thy will be done," or "I offer everything else to the universe."

Likewise in looking at one's self, it is possible to judge, fix and evaluate only to the extent that is normal and usual, and then say "I accept," or "Thy will be done," or "I offer everything else to the universe."

And if you find dissatisfaction with your own ability to be freely, try this:

1. Accept your craziness—completely.
2. Accept your dissatisfaction with being crazy—completely.
3. Accept your attempts to do something about it—completely.
4. Accept your inability to accept whatever you cannot accept—completely.

VIII. *ATTENTIVENESS*

Awareness is the nutrient field in which sanity will grow. Sometimes it is possible to encourage free awareness by being attentive. Attentiveness is different from paying attention. In paying attention some things are blocked out so that awareness can be focused on one thing. In attentiveness, nothing is blocked. One is open to all that is.

One can try to keep as sharply aware as possible, in all the things one does—not so that one can be in better control, but just to *see*. In order to nurture this attentiveness, one must find a way of being relaxed and alert simultaneously. At times this may seem like going against old habits, in which relaxation means dullness and alertness means tension. But relaxing with bright awareness can happen. And one might do well to encourage it.

Become aware of *now*. Bring awareness gently into the full immediate present. Whenever tension occurs, whenever some fantasy or worry has carried your attention "away," simply blink your eyes and see what is, right here, right now. Be sharp, clear, bright. Do nothing which will dull awareness.

Sometimes with immediate awareness, a judging parental quality will develop. It will evaluate and label, worry and plan. And it will capture awareness again, kidnapping it from the here and now. When this happens it seldom can be fought. But if one can take one more step back and *see* the judging happening, awareness will then remain bright and present. No matter what is going on, it is possible to be aware, right now.

In all things, be aware now. Watch your movements, how they flow from one to the next. Watch your hands move. Eating, talking, working, see it all happening in that very moment. In the middle of a busy day, listen to your breathing. Be aware of the beating of your heart. When any sound stops, listen to the silence. In listening to music, let your breathing go with it.

Try keeping a thought, word, image or prayer going somewhere in your mind all the time. Listen to it whenever you can. And if you must pay attention, pay attention to your immediate being, to the consciousness you share with all creation.

IX. *SPACE*

Sense space. Sense openness. Find spaciousness in every situation. Begin perhaps with sensing the physical space around you, between you and someone else. Then sense space between you and your feelings and experiences. But then allow the idea of you to pass away. Then only spaciousness, in and through and around everything, remains.

X. *TIME*

Let each moment, as it strikes you, be totally fresh and new. Make no extra connections of yourself with past or future. In planning or remembering, simply see that it's occuring now. There is no need to struggle into an awareness of now. No need to get into the immediate moment. You are already there, and all it takes is relaxing to realize it.

XI. *LEARNING*

Learning springs from being. One does not learn to be. The making of concepts is like a work of art, an attempt to express or describe experience. Concepts should never dictate experience. They should only reflect it. Thus approach life without conception, totally open to what may be.

If you should move to sacrifice concepts, be sure to sacrifice the concept of being without concepts.

If you learn from books or teachings, reading the Bible or the Talmud, the Sutras or the Gita, let the words flow into you as if they were raindrops to nourish your soul. You need not pull the words into yourself. Simply let your spirit drink. And when you speak, to teach others or to paint a word picture of

being, you need not push the words out. Let them flow forth
from you as from a spring.

XII. *COMPASSION*

Remember to look for compassion rather than make it.
Find love rather than build it. When you discover it, simply
watch.

In your doing, do compassionate things. Do loving acts.
But do not confuse this with love.

XIII. *PRAYER*

If you do pray:

1. Pray
2. Do the best you can
3. Accept the whole situation
4. Watch with awe

If you don't pray:

1. Do the best you can
2. Accept the whole situation
3. Watch with awe

If you can't pray:

1. Do the best you can
2. Accept the whole situation
3. Watch with awe
4. Be still and listen

If prayer happens, watch who's praying. Sometimes it seems like you praying, and sometimes it doesn't. Listen to noisy prayer. And listen to quiet prayer. And if there's no prayer at all, listen to that.

XIV. *HUMOR*

If you don't try to make light of things but simply find the humor which is there, self-importance is eased without pain. It is helpful to seek out the humor in everything you do—perhaps even to write down the most heroic, tragic, painful, nostalgic, meaningful, important things in your life and look for their funniness.

XV. *WAITING*

Practice the deep, quiet art of waiting. In making decisions, if a direction seems right, follow it. But if nothing seems right, wait. Wait for rightness. If there is no time to wait, move ahead to do whatever is the best you can do. *Then* wait.

And in living, do not rush your sanity. Do the best you can. Then wait.

12

THE FEAR
OF
SANITY

Death in itself is nothing; but we fear
To be we know not what, we know not where.

John Dryden, *Aurengzebe*

Sanity does not come without a price. Or at least a feeling of a price. The price itself is the death of delusion, and the direct experience of the price is fear.

There is a strange fearsomeness about giving up into life, going beyond self-control, listening to sanity. It is not quite like any other fear that humans can experience. In it, all the opposites of life are swirled together: living and dying, belonging and abandonment, power and impotence, joy and dread. This is a fear worth seeing very closely.

The fear of freely sanely being is made up of a series of layers. For most people the outer layers all have to do with losing control. At first the fear of losing control may take on a rather fleeting psychological flavor. "If I let my mind be—my feelings—my fantasies, maybe I'll find out that I'm basically crazy." Or perhaps there is fear of experiencing some feelings one does not wish to have. Scary feelings. Petty jealousies. Revenge. Rage. Fanatacism. Or, worse yet, mediocrity. But soon one realizes that in accepting one's own awful qualities, one can also accept their natural suppression, and relaxation can happen again. It may even turn out that one's insides are not as horrible as they had seemed.

One of the fears associated with loss of control, then, is of self-discovery. Or more precisely of discovering certain *qualities* of self. Finding out the true attributes of who one is and perhaps discovering that they're not very nice. Going beyond self-control means to confront one's images of one's self very directly. To relax the barriers against perception and to be open to what is. There are times when to do this begins to feel like great unpleasantness.

Another layer of fear is that of disappointment and unintended sacrifice. Giving up control of self means that perhaps one will not get what one wants. Or that perhaps one will get what one doesn't want. Perhaps one will not have any fun. There is a sense of risk-taking here. It is not a very deep or heavy fear, but it plays its part in making people defensive against sanity.

Then a deeper layer of fear is encountered. "If I give up control and allow myself to be, will someone or something take over? Who or what will it be? And can it be trusted?"

This fear is born in the delusional idea that in order for there to be control, one must somehow do the controlling. A friend of mine named Bill described this rather graphically. "I was sitting quietly, letting my whole being relax. Things became superbly quiet. It was wonderful. I became aware that the only thing left which I could identify as 'me' was a little observer, just passively watching everything. The peace was incredible, and there was great beauty there, beyond all words. But there was another feeling as well. A deep, creeping dread. Here was my life, JUST GOING ON! Breathing happening, heart beating, birds outside singing, sounds of traffic in the background, and it was all SIMPLY TAKING PLACE! I got this idea that someone else, somewhere else, just had to be *doing* all that. And I got so scared I started to shake, and before I could identify what was happening the peace just evaporated. I became very conscious of myself again, and then I wasn't scared anymore. But the beauty was gone."

Bill realized, intellectually, that his fear was both natural and unfounded at the same time. He recognized that what he had experienced was the "fear and trembling" so often described by those who have perceived the sense of some universal process. He said "It's just that I've been so used to holding the reins of my life. I feel naked if I ease my grip at all." But he'd also had the feeling that someone or something else was taking over, and that was somehow even more terrifying. "Maybe if I knew it was God," he said, "if I could name it God and believe in its benevolence, it wouldn't be so frightening. But I don't know what God is. And what if it's not God? What if it's evil?"

This is the fear of ultimate vulnerability. People usually deal with this fear in one of three ways. First, they may become so frightened that they retreat with great haste to the more comfortable and familiar world of managing their own destinies. But if they realize that in the process of managing their own lives they still cannot be certain about good and evil, they may seek out a faith. If this faith is fairly strong, they can enter into sanity with a simple prayer. Even without a clear sense of to whom they're praying, they can say, "Thy will be done." But if the faith is not so strong, their trust in benevolence not so great, they may enter sanity through the doorway of despair. "I know I can't manage it all. And I don't know who's going to. Still, there is no choice but for me to give up to what is. Whatever it is. I can hope it will be good, but good or bad, I shall have to accept it."

The fear of whether control will be assumed by something good or evil is understandable enough, but beneath this question lies another terror. What if there's nobody there at all? Can things simply take place, happen, *be*, without anyone doing it at all? Can it all just go on, like some cosmic perpetual motion machine, just happening, all by itself?

This is the next layer: a fear of aloneness. Of abandonment. A woman described it to me this way. "It was like I was an astronaut in outer space, and my lifeline had just broken. I was drifting deeper and deeper into emptiness, free, swirling voidness, totally silent. I was so terribly, terribly alone. I was afraid I'd just drift out there and never get back. Just stay there, nowhere, forever. I don't think I've ever been so scared. Still, it was so beautiful."

Many of these fears have a very familiar ring to many people. In one way or another, to a greater or lesser extent, nearly everyone has experienced them. So these are very natural fears. Yet they all come from delusion. They are all basically unfounded. The fear of vulnerability to evil, for example, is a myth because if one simply sacrifices one's attempts to control the self, one in no way kills one's own inner sense of rightness and wrongness. One simply allows whatever sense of good and evil one has, to be there. And thus one remains as capable of distinguishing right from wrong as ever. One simply ceases the struggle of continually trying to improve upon this ability. In allowing one's self to be, one cannot cast discretion to the winds. One simply allows it to be what it is.

And the feeling of abandonment is also mythical. It means that one is convinced that one is somebody distinct and irrevocably separated from the rest of the world, and thus capable of *being* abandoned. Sanity itself would be reassuring. If heard, it would be saying, "You are at one with the world. You always have been and always shall be. How then can you be abandoned?"

And the image of drifting helplessly into a void is also just as crazy. The woman who described this experience had in fact been sitting in a meditation group when it happened. She was in a real room full of real people. And she wasn't really drifting anywhere. She was right there all the time. The experience she had was just a projection of her fear. Simply an image of her fear of losing a sense of self-in-relation-to-others.

But to hear that these fears are unfounded, to recognize their unreality with one's intellect, does not at all mean that the fears will cease. All this knowledge does is allow one to perceive the fear with a sense of space. To see the fear more for what it is as it occurs, rather than being totally captured by it.

Each person has his or her own configuration of fear-layers. For some, loss of control is most prominent. For others, loneliness and abandonment. But for all of us, the fears have times of seeming very, very real. And they cannot be bypassed. Moving through one's own layers of fear is a sort of purification, the sacrifice of pieces of delusion. It is this which accounts for the strange quality with which fear of sanity is imbued. It is this which makes fear of sanity unlike any other kind of fear. The fear of sanity is always associated with beauty. None of its terror occurs without a background of great wonder, and never does one experience its dread without an aura of peace. Thus it is a sweet sort of panic that one experiences as the layers of fear are peeled away and the voice of sanity is heard more clearly.

As one comes closer to the center of these layers, it becomes evident that all the fears are simple manifestations of a single basic dread. This is the core-anxiety: Nonbeing. Death. One realizes that each of the layers of fear has been one aspect of the sense of self screaming for survival. Delusion sensing the threat of direct scrutiny and pleading for its life.

One may have habitually associated the sense of self with control, or with management, or with relationship, or with the satisfaction of desire. These predilections will determine which of the specific fears are most terrifying to the individual. But since nearly everyone has come to associate self with *being*, the loss of delusion always seems like death at core. The final acceptance of sanity requires a realization that being simply is. That there need be no separate "one" who is *doing* the process of being. To lose one's self in order to find one's self, to die in order to be reborn; these are not empty propositions. They are not simple platitudes. There are times for everyone when they feel very real.

Those times, when death looms most realistically, ironically occur when life is most fully perceived. It is in deeply sensing our existence that we most completely fear death. Looking deeply into the immediate functioning of one's mind, watching thoughts rise and fall, or acutely sensing emotion, or breathing beauty deeply, this is when one is most likely to sense, "I AM." And the more vibrantly one senses "I AM," the more vivid is the awareness that "I MIGHT NOT BE."

A colleague of mine, after experiencing some considerable fear in watching his mind at work, had a memory. "I remember having this kind of fear when I was a little kid. Maybe about five or so. When I first realized that I was thinking. And I suddenly became aware that I *was*. And right then—immediately, came this tremendous fear. 'If I *am*, then it's possible that I might *not be*.' "

It is in fully perceiving life that one comes to fear death the most. This is, of course, the brink of sanity. One more step and life is no longer perceived as by an observer, but lived, by a participant. And at that point self is no longer defined. Death of self-image has occurred. But of course nothing has really died. Just a mistaken idea, replaced by the truth.

If it is in fully perceiving life that one most vividly fears death, it is no wonder that humankind tends to kill awareness of being in so many ways. It is no wonder why we walk dazedly through so much of life. And why full appreciation of being is reserved for moments now and then. Moments we have come to call "peak experiences." This continual suppression of awareness is simply one of many defenses humankind uses against the fear of sanity. It is a form of repression, more deep and pervasive than any of the private psychological repressions described by Freud and his followers.

The story of humanity's attempts to avoid sanity does in fact read like a psychological case history. Humankind went crazy in its youth and now fights to preserve delusion in its maturity. Great energy is expended to avoid the fear of fully being. It is as if sanity were a driving force within mankind, like sex or aggression. More gentle perhaps, but even more powerful and threatening.

Psychotherapists are familiar with the threats of sexuality and aggression, and with the defense mechanisms people use to counteract these threats. But seldom has psychotherapy identified the threat of sanity and the defenses used against it. People *repress* sanity repeatedly by shoving it totally out of their consciousness, diving into the depths of delusion in order to avoid fear. And they *displace* sanity, seeking union, meaning, fulfillment in every conceivable way *except* in fully freely being. And they *project* their fear of sanity onto other people, labeling as "fanatic" anyone who proclaims to have experienced deeply living. And they *isolate* sanity, separating ideas *about* it from the experience *of* it, spending their efforts talking and writing about life rather than living it.

As a matter of fact, fully freely being has been more repressed and distorted than either sexuality or aggression. It has been, in recent generations, a taboo more pervasive than the taboo of sexuality in the Victorian era. The deep openness of life, the meaning of being, the experience of God were things one simply did not speak about openly. They were considered more private and personal than one's bedroom. It is only recently that America has begun to emerge from this age of spiritual Victorianism and has started to affirm, however tentatively, the personal search for being completely alive.

Now, as one might expect, people are beginning to talk

excessively about it. About consciousness and being, awareness and transcendence, spirituality and mysticism. As usual, the pendulum will probably swing too far. It *is* better sometimes to keep quiet about these things. But not out of fear. Simply out of the realization that words don't work. And that words are dangerous. For as we know so well by now, words often get substituted for the reality they attempt so poorly to describe.

There is one other aspect of defensiveness against sanity which should be mentioned. It has to do with a kind of self-determining "backlash." Several months ago I was participating in a retreat with a group of people who, like myself, were busily trying to freely be. Of course we didn't get very far with it because we were trying so hard to do it. But there were times. Times of open acceptance of what is. Times when the trying stopped and being started. Several weeks later, one of the participants told me of his experience. "While I was on the retreat I felt wonderful. I really felt like I was able to let myself be. More than ever before. I thought it was a great experience. But now I'm not so sure. Because as soon as the retreat was over I found I was trying to commandeer my life more than ever. It seemed like I was worse off than when I started. I don't know what to make of it."

As we talked, it became clear that even though he'd felt no great fear consciously during the retreat, his sense of self apparently had been threatened considerably by the experience of freely being. And in his response after the retreat, it seemed that his sense of self was making up for lost time by demonstrating how very powerful it could be.

Part of the problem here may have been that he had pushed himself a bit much on the retreat. The usual mistake of trying hard to "just be." And he had later paid a price for his hard-pushing of himself. But the other factor was that there were times when he really did relax, and he really did begin to ease his grip on the controls over himself, and that resulted in a backlash. Sometimes, after an experience of just being, the pendulum swings back and life seems more controlled than ever.

With this understanding, it might be possible to find a bit of compassion for self-centeredness and egocentrism in oneself and others when it occurs. For example, it had always been a mystery to me that certain people who proclaimed to be on a "spiritual" path sometimes appeared to be extremely self-concerned. Where I presumed they "ought" to be interested in selfless giving to others, they appeared far more interested in their own personal image. I used to react with rage when I encountered this. It seemed so hypocritical. But perhaps this self-centeredness is simply the backlash of a very threatened ego. Perhaps it is something those people needed to go through. Perhaps it is something that *can* be gone through, for any of us.

At this point, I feel it is necessary to repeat a warning. As I indicated at the very outset, one of the most destructive tendencies in the human condition is that as soon as one identifies an imperfection, one wants to fix it. And the fixing requires more fixing. Having just proclaimed that people all over the world are busily distorting and repressing sanity, I now fear that there will be a desire to do something to remedy the situation. Nothing is more likely to lead one away from awareness of being. Let us simply be aware of the way things are, the good and the bad, and allow that awareness to move through us toward healing. Nothing special need be done. And nothing special need not be done.

The fear of sanity creates a lively process for discovery of being. The fact that the fear is not founded in reality does not in the least detract from its energy. At times it is easy to take this fear very seriously. And, in the sense of delusion, it is serious. It really does mean death of one's sense of substantial and important self. But in the sense of sanity, there is some delightful humor in our struggle against dying.

Suddenly discovering that one is experiencing a "peak" of

being, a union, a peace beyond words, there occurs a recognition. "Wow, this is beautiful. This is a great experience." And as suddenly as it came, the experience slips away. Why? Because the sense of self has been deeply threatened and it becomes very sneaky. It says, "This is such a wonderful, blissful experience, I want to keep it forever." In the guise of "wanting to keep it," one very subtly gets back in control. And of course the experience is destroyed. There is truly marvelous humor in this treachery.

Or in simply watching one's self trying to stop trying or working at relaxing, it becomes very difficult not to giggle. And if a giggle is permitted, a guffaw is usually close on its heels. And if *that* is permitted, being may become free in spite of oneself.

13

FAITH,
PRAYER
AND TRUST

Know you what it is to be a child? It is to
be something very different from the man of
today. It is to have a spirit yet streaming
from the waters of baptism; it is to believe
in love, to believe in loveliness, to believe
in belief. . .

Francis Thompson

Fear of losing control, of vulnerability, and of abandonment
rest like cloaks over the basic anxiety of nonbeing. Taken together these fears are simply too fierce for most people to handle unarmed and undefended. It is a heroic image to think of
facing self-loss nakedly, with total vulnerability. But of course
heroism is very seductive. One is tempted to feel "I am being
heroic in my holiness. I have faced the ultimate fear of nonbeing. My soul is on the mountain, whipped by universal winds,
alone, triumphant I have met the universe and lived!" And of
course this simply helps to reestablish the importance of one's
image of one's self.

So for most people it is both humble and necessary to
think that when they give up control of self there is someone or
something to give up *to*. It is only from the deepest despair
that one can give up totally to nothing at all. Most people have
a real need to say "Thy will be done."

Even though this approach raises interminable questions about who or what takes control, and whether the new controller is basically benevolent or sinister, it still seems more comfortable to give up to something than simply to cast one's self to the winds of a chaotic void.

This is where a concept of God becomes important. To be sure, all concepts about God are wrong. Just as one's concepts of other people can never substitute for the people themselves. In deep meeting with other people, one senses that no concept, no matter how wise, could ever capture their essence. And of course the same is true of a concept of God.

But the fallibility of a God-concept does not lessen people's *need* for such a concept. Nor does it keep people from treating a concept as the real thing for a while. If one is deeply frightened, deeply pained and in great need of reassurance, one has neither the time nor the energy to cogitate about the fallibility of concepts. One simply grabs hold of a concept and uses it the best way one can. And sometimes it is just as necessary to have someone or something to thank when life has been especially beautiful. If one needs to say "Help" or "Thank you," one simply needs to say it, and often one needs a sense of someone or something to say it to. If one needs to pray, it often seems that a concept will do, in lieu of the "real thing."

It's a kind of idolatry to worship or pray to a concept. But sometimes, especially during the process of giving up self-control, concept-idolatry becomes imperative. The feeling may be, "Here I go, slipping, falling under, losing my grip, opening up, allowing, and I'm *scared*." Then words seem to come. "Dear God, protect me." "Holy Mary, Mother of God." "Lord Krishna, guide me." "Allah protect me." "Our Father who art in heaven . . ." Voices speaking the concept-names of God in fear. The fact that the words themselves are determined by culture is unimportant. The feeling is that one needs help and needs it *now*.

Faith plays a very important role here, for up to a point the stronger one's faith is, the easier it is to let go. Up to the point of letting go of faith itself and allowing it to grow into trust. But since faith is as much a gift as love, it matters little to know that faith can ease fear. One "has" only as much faith as one is aware of. Like love, more faith cannot willfully be manufactured.

It is usually assumed that people need faith in order to pray. But this is not necessarily true. For many people, both faith and prayer seem immature, weak, childish. And faith is willfully disavowed. But prayer keeps popping up. Like sanity, it is almost never totally repressible. It may be disguised and distorted, but it keeps slipping out. And sometimes prayer without faith can really be what nurtures sanity into fruition.

A young man named Michael gave his account. "My family was pretty religious, and I used to pray a lot as a kid. But after I got into college I began to realize that faith was a crutch and prayer was just evidence of being immature—not being able to stand up for yourself. So I canned the whole business. I just shucked all the religious stuff and set about to live as fully and constructively as I could. Now and then, when I was really scared, or when I wanted something very badly, a stupid little prayer would squeak out. Like I'd find myself whispering, "Dear God . . ." But I'd squelch it quick, because it embarrassed me. Nobody heard it, but I was still embarrassed. It didn't fit my image of myself.

"Then several years ago I got into meditation. It started out as a trip. I just wanted to see what it was like. But after a while, I began to sense something—like a different way of being that might be possible. I can't really describe it, but I got more serious about meditating. As that happened, I started going 'deeper,' letting myself go more fully, opening up and letting be. And I got more and more frightened. I'd feel my controls loosening, my image of myself just slipping away.

Then one day the fear got so bad it literally forced words of prayer out of me. Since I had no viable concept of God, the first prayers were very sophisticated, like 'Oh universe, all your chaotic tumbling randomness, help me. Let the chips fall where they may, but I hope the chips fall in such a way that I won't be destroyed.' "

He chuckled as he said this, aware of the great lengths to which he'd gone in order to avoid anything sounding the least bit religious.

"Then after a while, it seemed like it just took too much energy to come up with all the big words, so the 'prayer' shortened itself to 'Power of the cosmos, protect me,' or 'Sequence of events, be kind.' " He grinned as he continued. "Finally I just gave up and the prayer became, 'O.K., God, whoever or whatever you are, thy will be done.' See, it had dawned on me that my talking to the universe was no different from talking to God. I was just using different words. I remembered times when I had silently thanked a tree for being beautiful or silently asked a girl to fall in love with me. It was all the same. I'd been praying all the time anyway. Just without any concept of God. Anyway, with this realization I was able to let prayer happen and not be ashamed of it. I had no faith about it. It just happened. After this, prayer came more freely. Not like I was *doing* it, but rather that I'd given it permission to happen. Prayer kept happening when I was afraid, and there was something about it that eased the fear just a little. But I also found myself praying when I wasn't afraid—when I was happy or sort of celebrating.

"I used to think people made up God out of their fear. Now I don't think that's quite right. Maybe fear makes the concepts of God, and maybe fear can propel prayer into your consciousness, but it's more like prayer was there all the time. It was just a part of who I was, and I wasn't aware of it. And the concepts of God are just tools or ways of making it easier.

But the source of prayer and the nature of God are basically beyond any doing or labeling that I can accomplish. If I need a certain concept of God from time to time, that's O.K. I can use it—maybe even treat it as absolute when it's necessary. But all along, underneath, I can know it's really beyond me. Somehow with that approach I'm not embarrassed by prayer anymore. I don't feel I'm copping out. I'm just letting me be."

As Michael discovered, concepts of God or of a universal process can act as a kind of bridge between total in-control self-determination and total openness and acceptance of what is. Any kind of faith can be a bridge in this way. A help in transition. Something to mediate a transformation, so that one does not have to leap from delusion into sanity with no hand-holds at all. So that one need not go totally naked into the awesome openness of sanity. So that one does not necessarily have to endure the treachery of heroism.

When Michael was in college he saw faith and prayer as crutches and he cast them off. Now he may still see faith as a crutch, but he recognizes that there are times, for him, when such a crutch may be necessary. There is a place for crutches. When one looks across a lake on a bright summer day, one shields one's eyes from the sun. This is using a crutch. Climbing up a steep hill, one grasps at branches and rocks to keep from slipping. This is also a crutch. Yet one does not feel guilty or embarrassed about it. There is no special credit to be gained by *not* shielding one's eyes from the sun or grasping handholds on a hill.

But a crutch is always used in transition. It helps one travel from one place to another, or to change from one perception to another, and there comes a time when the crutch is no longer necessary. In the transition between delusion and sanity, the crutch of faith becomes transformed. Faith turns into trust. Trust based on the solid experience of having repeatedly allowed one's self to be. Then there is less frantic grasping for concepts and more calm acceptance of what is. No need to invent beliefs. No need to cling to one's faith. No need to prepare concepts with which to face the experience of living.

As the experience of God deepens, there is less need for a concept of God. As reality is met more closely, ideas *about* reality can be relinquished. As life is more openly accepted, there is less need to think about living. And as one moves more intimately into the fear of nonbeing, self-protection can be eased. Then concepts fall back into their more natural place. Rather than being idols substituting for reality, concepts become works of art, attempts to communicate reality rather than prescribe it.

At this point, the disputes between one concept and another seem petty and irrelevant. This faith or that, science or religion, spirit or psyche are meaningless. To struggle with religion or faith or prayer or God becomes a waste of energy. The realization dawns that sanity is spiritual. It simply is. Like the primeval man's unity with nature, there is no question about it. No need to figure it out, explain it or defend it in any way.

It all, just simply, is.

14

SEVENTEEN YEARS LATER

And all manner of things shall be well.

Julian of Norwich

Seventeen years later it is still true: "It all, just simply, is." That sentence still sums it up perfectly for me, and in some ways it hardly seems right to add to it. The way things simply are, however, involves the way things are *becoming*, and there have been some changes in seventeen years. In this chapter and the next, I want to describe some developments that have taken place in my own thinking and in our culture's attitude toward basic sanity. There will be nothing wholly new in what follows, only a little elaboration that may bring the old words up-to-date.

In re-reading the old words, I asked myself what I might change if I were writing them today. In truth I found nothing of substance that I really disagreed with, no basic ideas I felt were wrong. As I said in the Preface, however, today I would try to write in complete sentences instead of fragments, avoid masculine pronouns, and be more explicit about my own religious faith. I would also use more modern examples to illustrate my points. In addition, there are two themes I feel need further development.

A DEEPER MEANING OF PEACE AND SELF

In the first chapter, I quoted Joseph Conrad's statement that what people most long for is some form or formula of peace. Over the years, I have come to believe that love, not peace, is the primary human motivation. At first this might seem like a basic difference, for love is certainly not always peaceful. At the very least, love makes us ache. More likely, it leads us to the greatest pains life can hold. Love challenges us toward liberation, justice and creativity, and it draws us into levels of honesty and relinquishment that can be truly agonizing. If peace were all we were seeking we might be spared such agony, but our lives would stagnate, become dry and empty. Clearly this is not the nature of human life.

But we all *do* long for peace. The question, it seems to me, is what peace really means. I think we yearn for peace not as an end or final goal in life, but as a means toward greater fullness of living. In this sense, peace means spiritual freedom: a freedom not only from conflict and disharmony, but also a freedom *for* love, creation, healing and growth. We want to be free from impediments not so we can simply rest, but so we can get on with the essential business of our lives, which is love.

This larger way of understanding peace is in keeping with the biblical Hebrew word *shalom*. *Shalom* is usually translated as peace, but it means much more than just absence of conflict. It implies wholeness, completeness and fullness of life. The early Christian theologian Irenaeus referred to such wholeness when he proclaimed that "the glory of God is a human being fully alive." With this more full meaning of peace, Joseph Conrad's words make much more sense. What we really long for is *shalom*.

Similarly, a more comprehensive understanding of my references to "self" would be helpful. In the early work, I emphasized the delusion of seeing the self as an object, a thing to be built and fixed. Today I am just as convinced as ever of the destructiveness of such thinking. To see ourselves and one another in this way is malignant; it kills life-spirit. So I still feel the suggestion in Chapter 11 to "Forget worrying about who you are" is some of the best advice I have ever given. In re-reading the book, however, I felt that some of my words might seem to devalue the human self or even to deny its existence. Because so many people in our culture do suffer a devaluing of self-sense, some elaboration is needed.

We *are* selves, and these selves-that-we-are are absolutely real, amazingly unique, indescribably beautiful and wondrously precious. The trick about our selves, however, is that they are also endlessly mysterious. We can never catch hold of them, never capture their nature. This is why we miss our reality and even damage one another when we think of ourselves as things. Whenever we try to objectify ourselves, we blunder over the elusive wonder of who we really are; we diminish our reality.

Here I want to recover another old Hebrew word: *nephesh*. It is usually translated as "soul," and it means the essence of a person, the fundamental nature of who one is. The biblical understanding is that soul is true self, real self—not something we possess but who we truly are. In this sense, soul is a very definite reality, not something esoteric or ethereal. It is our person-being, not separate from our physical bodies yet not limited to them. Soul, self, is a fabric spun from infinite life yet inextricably woven into the earth and all creation.

Over the past seventeen years, the increasing influence of women's wisdom and the blessed re-emergence of reverence for creation have helped our culture become more receptive to such a soul-sense of ourselves. In developing a greater appreciation of the mysterious beauty of nature, we have been able to accept more deeply our own mystery—the precious beauty of our souls. This, in turn, is nurturing our basic sanity. We can now more easily sense the value of simply being. We can at least entertain the notion of letting ourselves be. We are, however, not there yet.

THE INTERVENING YEARS: PSYCHOTHERAPY

We have a long way to go. Our culture's addiction to self-building and self-fixing continues. Transpersonal psychology is no longer "the newest field of psychotherapy," as I called it in the original text. Every other year, another new field emerges. In the past two decades, countless new forms of therapy have developed within the mental health professions. On the popular front, many people still want to see the best new insights as the ultimate fix. When I wrote *Simply Sane,* the "in" things were meditation, biofeedback, psychedelic drugs, est, and the like. In the intervening years we have seen frenzies of personality typing, as in the Myers–Briggs Type Inventory and the Enneagram, and an onslaught of Twelve-Step recovery groups for addiction, codependency, adult children, and now early childhood abuse. The good thing about such waves of interest is that they always contribute something worthwhile to our appreciation of ourselves—if they did not contain some truth, they would not become so popular. We always press them too far, however; we take them beyond their limited truths in our grasping for self-control. We are still seeking the quick fix; we are still laboring under the delusion that we can and should control our selves. Still, I am convinced this attitude is softening. The dying-and-resurrecting I hoped for in the early chapters is really taking place.

As with all death and resurrection, it may seem at first that things are getting worse. The American health care system of the 1990s is a hard example. The sledgehammer of economics has forced mental health services into ever greater objectification. In many ways, the personhood of people has never been more ignored. But there is a breath of grace in this darkness, a hint of resurrection among the bones. By being forced to the extreme, the way health care systems disregard and disparage people's souls has become obvious. No longer able to deny such dehumanization, many health care professionals are feeling very uneasy. Most entered the field because somewhere in their hearts they really wanted to connect with people's souls in helpful ways. Now they are realizing what a luxury and privilege that is, and how it is not the same thing as solving people's problems. In other words, by being forced to deal more and more technically with people's objective problems, they are experiencing a softer, gentler reverence for people's souls.

Finally, I sense a kind of rightness—albeit incomplete—in the growing focus on technically efficient problem-solving. In our culture at least, this has always been the proper business of health care systems, and the more we can develop efficient ways to "fix" broken bones, cancer, or paralyzing depression and psychosis, the better. It is sad when such efficiency is accompanied by disrespect and uncaring for people, but at least our technological expertise is being brought to bear where it should be—on fixing things that need fixing—and we professionals have less opportunity to mess with people's souls. In this regard, I am generally gratified to see that behavior therapy, short-term, problem-oriented interventions, and appropriate use of medication are replacing the old endless psychotherapies that promised basic personality restructuring. I am pleased to see the establishment of specialized treatment centers for addictions, eating disorders, phobias and the like. To me, this means we are directing our expertise where it should properly go, and leaving people's selves alone. In a painful way, health care is being forced back to the basic simplicity of healing I described in Chapter 8: to restore things to a more natural state, to cleanse and purify, and to provide rest.

But what then happens to people's selves and souls? Are we as a culture just forgetting them entirely? On the contrary; from the standpoint of real mental health, I think the most wonderful thing happening in our culture is that people are beginning to take responsibility for their own sense of themselves. It has become increasingly obvious that no psychiatrist, no psychologist, no priest or guru or gimmick will be able to give us what our souls really need. Although the realization may at first seem disappointing, it opens the way to a deeper, more authentic appreciation of the mystery of our being. What our souls really need *is* available; it has always been and always will be available. It is given, being given, all the time. All it takes to recognize and appreciate this gift is to ease our frantic striving to make it happen. In other words, to fully receive the gift, we have to at least try to trust that it is being given. We need to give it a chance.

Outside the systems of mental health care, many things are happening that point in the direction of this basic sanity. As just a few examples, I think of the growing appreciation of myth as evidenced by the popularity of Joseph Campbell's work, the recovery of story and archetype in the offerings of Clarissa Pinkola Estés, the re-seeking of personal values and civil responsibility addressed by M. Scott Peck, the claiming of deep wisdom and spirit in what it means to be woman and man, our growing respect for nature, the fresh appreciation of Native American and other primal spiritualities, and, for that matter, the increasing openness of both our secular and religious systems to the very *idea* of spirituality.

I could go on with examples, but understand me here: none of these movements will ever be *the* answer, and if we try to make them so we will fall back into the old trap of self-fixing and soul-building. The fundamental goodness of such movements is not that they give us health and wholeness, but that they help point us in that direction; they orient us toward the gift-already-being-given. They encourage our open-eyed trust in the essential goodness of creation, of Creator, of ourselves. In one way or another, they are all saying that what our souls need is indeed a gift, not something to achieve, accomplish, or otherwise make happen artificially. They are affirming that the human self is not something for building or fixing, but a beautiful, whole being to be lived. Listen, for example, to these words from Clarissa Pinkola Estés:

> To return to an alert innocence is not so much an effort, like moving a pile of bricks from here to there, as it is standing still long enough to let the spirit find you. It is said that all you are seeking is also seeking you . . .[1]

Such wisdom is deeply encouraging. The word "encourage" literally means to put heart in, to give heart. Heart-giving is the real contribution of spiritually helpful insights and movements. Fundamentally, this encouragement is always toward the basic trustworthiness of who we are and what life is all about. I myself am deeply encouraged that so many people now seem much more ready to hear such wisdom, to really take it in and let it give heart to their own inherent sanity.

I have seen such encouragement happening among mental health professionals. I know from personal experience that these care-givers are among those who have been most wounded by the inhumanity of our systems and by the delusion of self-fixing. They often cover their woundedness with the professional armor of distance and objectivity, sometimes even harshness and bitterness. But in recent years I have seen the armor soften in many professionals. I have felt them become more willing to

---

[1]Clarissa Pinkola Estés. *Women Who Run With the Wolves* (New York: Ballantine, 1992), p. 152.

share their vulnerability and sense of inadequacy. In so doing, they open not only to a greater respect for their patients, but also to a more authentic and inherently natural soul-strength within themselves.

My first and most striking experience of this occurred not long after *Simply Sane* was first published. At the time there was a brief experiment in which a hotline was set up for people to call and talk anonymously about whatever was on their minds. The interesting thing was that they spoke only to an answering machine; they knew no one would respond to what they said. The experiment did not last long, but many people called and poured their hearts out to the answering machine. One was a psychiatrist who said, "I'm supposed to be helping people and I have no idea how. I don't know what I'm doing." When I read the report of this man's words, I understood him very well. Even though he was only talking to a machine, he was confessing a truth he felt, and it was a truth I had also felt.

When I was in medical training, most of the academic psychiatrists who supervised me seemed to have no such problem; they appeared to know exactly what to do and how to do it. They exuded absolute cold competence about fixing people, and I felt very ignorant in comparison to them. They had an answer to every question; the words "I don't know" never passed their lips. It took me a long time to realize that although they were indeed extremely competent in their field, there was much that they weren't sure about. They just could not admit it to their patients or colleagues, or, I believe, even to themselves. Not long ago I had the opportunity to meet some of these men and women again. They had changed. Now approaching retirement, they were far more gentle and open, vulnerable, humbly able to admit the limits of their expertise. What touched me most was their reverence for mystery and their desire to learn more about the spiritual dimension of life for themselves as well as their patients.

As young people mature, they often go through a transition in which their parents and teachers suddenly seem much wiser than they used to, but my experience with these psychiatrists was different. Some of these men and women have really changed, deep in their hearts. I had a long talk with one of them, during which he said, "Of course I have always cared about my patients—all physicians do, in their own way—but caring was mostly a means of doing my job. Compassion used to be a technique, like the therapeutic attitude we call 'unconditional positive regard.' Now it's different. Patients still come to me because they have difficulty functioning, but I know function isn't everything. There's something deeper that I need to be attentive to. I don't understand it and I don't know how to be with it, but it's something in people that makes me feel *really* loving, almost reverent."

I have seen this kind of change taking place in many professionals, young and old, throughout America and other countries, not only in mental health but in religion, business, even education and politics. Part of it is due to factors I have mentioned above—economy forcing people into bare-bones confrontations with what is really important. Part of it is because in many areas we have progressed far enough technologically to realize that technology is not going to answer everything. But there is more to it. In the face of modern challenges, people could just as easily become defensive, embittered and entrenched in their old ways. Why, instead, are so many becoming more humble, open, and searching for something deeper? Before, mystery was the enemy and professional competence the ideal. Why are people now developing a sense of reverence for the unknown and finding deep peacefulness in not knowing all the answers? From a Christian perspective, I can only say that the Holy Spirit is on the move. Grace is flowing with a particular kind of abundance, calling us more strongly and guiding us more clearly toward true healing and wholeness. Whatever words you might use, something is changing, and it is for the better. It is pointing toward trusting, basic sanity.

The recovery of basic sanity is painful, as healing often is. For professional therapists, it involves realizing two truths: human beings are not objects to be fixed; and when healing happens, it is not the therapist who "does" it. This is not easy to admit; it can threaten professional identity and financial livelihood as well. One therapist friend called me from the Midwest to say, "I don't know how long I can go on with this. People keep coming to me expecting me to put them back in order with quick efficient remedies, and I keep longing to encourage their souls. They have one agenda and I have another; I'm beginning to feel deceptive about it." Another told me, "I'm going to quit doing therapy altogether. Maybe I'll teach. As much as I love working with people, I feel like I'm riding a dinosaur with mental health care the way it is. It's time for me to get off."

Therapists who are encountering such difficulties feel very lonely. Even if their colleagues are beginning to feel the same thing, they are unlikely to admit it. It is a precious gift when two or more find each other and can begin to talk honestly about how they feel. Then, slowly, they recognize that their agony is not a symptom of something wrong but the necessary pain of their own healing, the death throes that precede resurrection.

Whether we are therapists or patients, whether we are homemakers or hermits, in some way we all need other people in the process of recovering our basic sanity. We need the encouragement, the heart-giving that others offer us simply by telling their own stories. This is yet another truth that more and more people are realizing: we cannot go it alone.

THE INTERVENING YEARS: MY JOURNEY

I have been blessed by the support of many friends and colleagues over the years as I tried to practice what I preached in the original chapters. In the process I did get off the dinosaur. Very gradually, almost without realizing it, I quit the practice of psychotherapy. It was not a conscious decision at all; for many years I kept trying to be true to my own sanity and to help people recover theirs within the existing systems and standards of health care. It was often difficult to be with people who could not believe in their own capacity for healing and therefore wanted me to fix them. It was also difficult to fit my understanding of human growth and healing into treatment plans with objective, problem-oriented goals. Still, my being with people did provide help for some of their problems as well as encourage their trust of themselves. I just put up with the frustrations.

On the surface, what happened seemed to be just a matter of scheduling. A few years after *Simply Sane* was published, I was invited to begin full-time work with the Shalem Institute for Spiritual Formation in Washington, D.C. In this setting I could teach, write, lead groups and retreats, and do further research. This meant I had to quit my hospital work, but I still tried to keep a small psychotherapy practice on the side. It quickly became evident that I did not have the time availability to prescribe medication and provide responsible monitoring of its effects. So I limited my practice to psychotherapy alone. As my work with Shalem expanded and involved more traveling, I could no longer even be available regularly enough for psychotherapy. On the surface, that is how I got off the dinosaur: a long, slow, slide.

At a deeper level, the less psychotherapy I did, the better I felt. I did not want to admit this to myself; I did not want to relinquish the professional credibility and personal identity that came from being a "practicing psychiatrist." But it was true. When I could be with people in spiritual companionship instead of psychotherapy we were so much more free from self-fixing expectations; the relief was indescribable. What a sense of liberation to be able to come together with others for the express purpose of making friends with the beautiful mystery of our being and seeking a deeper communion with the divine source of all growth, healing and love! This was what I had been looking for all my life. I had thought I would find it in psychotherapy, but it was not there. Psychotherapy was a step in my journey, and I had to move on.

In some ways—when I think about getting things "right" instead of simply being—I feel it was a mistake for me to go into psychiatry in the first place. What I really wanted was to be helpful to people at the deepest levels of their being. I wanted to be part of people's discovery of meaning, joy, love, and fundamental connectedness with the creative spirit of life. I made two mistakes about psychiatry. First, it was an error to believe that such a scientific/medical profession could effectively address the essential spiritual qualities of life. Second and more fundamental, my mistake was to believe that *any* profession could do so. Professions are roles determined by the values, standards, and expectations of society. As such, no profession, no role—not even a religious one—can adequately express our own basic sanity or enable us to help others find theirs. Psychiatrist, teacher, politician, gardener, parent, spouse, religious leader, homemaker: no such role will give us our truth. The truth must instead well up inside us, and when it does it will want to flow into our roles and *change* them. This will inevitably bring us into conflict with standards and expectations. This is the way life goes; when we think about getting things right, we see we have made many mistakes and errors. But essentially life is not about getting things right. It is about trusting the fundamental rightness that is inherent in life itself.

In truth I have no regrets about my twenty-five years of psychiatric practice. I am grateful for what it taught me and for the practical help I could give to people. Most of all, I am thankful for the opportunity to have been a witness to growth and healing in people's lives. Occasionally I even wonder if I might ever take up a clinical practice again. I certainly would not go back to doing insight-oriented or depth therapy. I have come to believe that such therapies are just not very helpful when either the therapist or the patient lacks a practical reverence for the soul's natural trustworthiness and an acknowledged dependency upon the divine for real healing and growth. I admire therapists who have the graceful stamina to maintain this attitude within themselves when their patients and the systems within which they work believe the opposite.

Even so, I question the propriety of such mixed agendas. I am not sure it is the therapist's job to try to correct a patient's self-fixing delusion if what the patient *really* wants is just to have a problem solved. If I want a broken bone set or an appendix removed, I do not contract with my physician for extra time and money to explore the existential meaning of my body parts. I believe many psychological disorders can and should be seen in the same way. When people simply want relief from pain or restoration of function, is that not what they should be offered if possible?

In this regard, I could return to psychiatry with integrity only as a technician. I could use behavioral techniques to help people overcome specific phobias or I could use medication to help people recover from depression. It could be simple, direct, uncomplicated. But in psychiatry, as in many other professions, one is virtually forced into a role. Now that I have tasted the precious freedom of role-less-ness in my work, I would not want to return to that particular struggle.

Work has been defined as the activities that help maintain life and household. By that definition, my work is indeed role-less. I fix things around the house, spend time with my family and friends, write, teach, talk with people, solve computer problems, mow the lawn, lead retreats and workshops, all without having to be anyone but me. I fully realize that I have been given a great gift in terms of my work in spirituality. In a world where people are homeless and starving, it is an almost unbelievable luxury to finally be able to make a living in a work so role-less and personally rewarding. But the gift of my work has helped me realize something that applies to all of us, no matter what our life circumstances. The truth is this: although we may find ourselves acting in many roles, *our roles do not need to define us.* We do not need to find our identity in work, in relationships, in social or economic conditions, in any such characterization of ourselves. Even if we try, we will never find who we truly are there. Moreover, we do not have to take inside ourselves the identities that others place upon us. With grace and courage, we can not only forget worrying about who we are; we can also forget worrying about who others think we are.

It may at first sound reassuring and hopeful to forget worrying about who we are. Ultimately, it *is* immensely reassuring. In practice, however, it is not at all easy and it takes considerable courage. As we worry less about defining ourselves according to roles, we relinquish hard, old, securing senses of who we are. This may leave us with a sense of not knowing who we are at all—a state of beginning sanity but one that can feel decidedly uncomfortable. Further, we risk disappointing others who may expect us to be living in predictable accordance with our roles. In many ways this can be even more threatening. Easing one's grip on a professional role can risk both status and livelihood. Ceasing to define oneself in terms of relational roles can threaten the relationships themselves.

It is not surprising, then, that we tend to cling to our roles and that our clinging can only ease gradually. Like all dimensions of recovering basic sanity, we neither can nor should expect ourselves to stop worrying about who we are all of a sudden. It needs to happen as it happens, as part of an ongoing process. Our participation in the process is not to make it happen, not to correct it, not even to boost it along, but to *allow* it, to give it freedom, space and gentle attentiveness. The process has a name, I think. It is called faith. And our participation in the process of faith also has a name: wise trust.

15

WISE TRUST

Where is the wisdom we have lost in knowledge?

T. S. Eliot

When I re-read the first thirteen chapters in preparation for this new edition, my strongest feeling was of wonder. It amazed me that even way back then I was so confident that God and the essential nature of life are completely good and absolutely trustworthy. Today I am even more confident of that truth, but sometimes I still wonder how I can be so sure. How can we believe that God is really trustworthy or that creation is really good when we see so much evil, injustice and needless suffering around us? For that matter, how can we trust our own basic sanity when we repeatedly see ourselves being selfish and un-loving?

I have explored these questions in many ways since *Simply Sane* first came out. In *Will and Spirit*, I looked at psychological willfulness, spiritual evil, and the theological issue of theodicy (how an all-good and all-powerful God can permit evil). In *Care of Mind/Care of Spirit*, I followed up on darkness, desolation and the demonic. In *Addiction and Grace*, I explored human enslavement by addiction and attachment. In *The Awakened Heart*, I investigated our fear of love and why love has to involve suffering. There are a lot of words in all these books, and I do think they help a little in making "sense" of things. But when all is said and done, the essential trustworthiness of life and self can neither be proven by words nor explained by concepts. It must be experienced, repeatedly. *And the trustworthiness can only be experienced by trusting it.* In simple, gentle little ways, we have to try to live as if it were true. Then the actual truth— which has been there all along—becomes increasingly apparent.

Over the years I have tried to live this way. I have tried to trust, to let myself be, to seek the divine One who is the source of all faith, hope and love. Over the years I have experienced the difference between trying to run my life with my own hands and letting myself be carried in the arms of a loving God. And, over the years, I have never once been let down by those arms. The goodness always comes through. Of course there have been many times when I didn't feel or recognize it, many times I have felt abandoned, even betrayed. But, given time, I have glimpsed the goodness in retrospect: God and God's creation are trustworthy. So what I said in Chapter 13 continues to come true for me: "faith turns into trust," and there is "no need to figure it out, explain it or defend it in any way."

Still there are countless times each day when I fail to trust and try to take things into my own hands again. After so many years, I really do not know why I continue to do this. If trying to live a trusting life were a matter of success or failure, I would be an abysmal failure. Yet the same thing happens to my friends and colleagues, so I guess it is human nature. In a strange way, I am happy for these many lapses, because each gives me a chance for *returning* to trust. I keep reenacting the story of the prodigal son, and it feels so good to keep coming home.

So I cannot prove the message of *Simply Sane* to you or to anyone. I can only encourage you to try it and test it. And because even the courage to try and test it must come as a gift, I ask you to pray for it. Pray for letting-be. Pray for simply being. Pray for trust. Pray for what you need. Pray for what God wants, even if you have not the slightest idea what that might be, or who or what God is. I am aware that I am now re-writing the last chapter of the original text. It still comes back to faith, prayer, and trust. So let me re-cycle these themes one more time, in the words I use today.

TRUST

First, our personal trust must be wise. By this I mean that blind trust is foolish; we need to try to discriminate between what is trustworthy and what is not. We must be wise as serpents yet innocent as doves. We must give ourselves to the essential goodness of life, but we also need to learn to read the signs of that goodness. This kind of discrimination is not a matter of logic or knowledge. It does not come to us through reading books or listening to erudite teachers. It comes to us through our own hearts, wounded and educated as they are through our life experience. It comes to us as a gift—sometimes it seems almost a presence—that is available to guide us through all of life's choices. It is the gift of wisdom.

Let me give you an example from my own life. In recent years I have discovered a deep reverence for nature, for the wilderness. I have read the literary masters of the wild: Thoreau, Whitman, London, Hubbard and the like. From a distance, I have tried to absorb something of the ancient wisdom of Native Americans and Australian Aborigines. But it is only in solitary experience in the wilderness itself that I have been given a clear sense of truly wise trust. The wilderness, like all of life, is full of beauty and full of danger. It is incredibly refreshing and nourishing, yet it can also kill you without a thought. Where, one might wonder, is the essential trustworthiness in this? With nature potentially deadly and our city streets even deadlier, it is not surprising that we give so much of our energy to protecting and securing ourselves that we develop almost paranoid attitudes toward life.

In my first expeditions into wilderness solitude, I too was almost paranoid, trying to prepare myself against all foreseeable dangers. I packed insect repellent and first aid equipment; I read up on snakes, poisonous plants and how to avoid being attacked by bears. My whole attitude was defensive. As I gained experience, however, the mountains and forests seemed to be sending· me a message. It was a message of gentleness, almost of hospitality. There was a truly *welcoming* atmosphere to the woods. It occurred to me that perhaps I could be more hospitable in return: aware of possible dangers yet open to the gentleness and gifts that the wilderness might offer. Since then, the wilderness has been my friend, one I treat with respect. I do not huddle in my tent for fear of snakes or bears, but neither do I run through the woods without looking where I am going. It is not necessary to be defensive, nor even to keep a list of dangers in mind all the time. All I need is to keep my eyes open, my senses alive. I think all of life is this way. If you protect yourself from all danger, you'll never really live. On the other hand, if you believe there is no danger at all, you may not live too long.

Slowly, I am bringing this attitude back into the city with me when I return from the mountain forests. I know it is very simple reasoning, but sometimes we must be reminded that the fundamental truths of life are simple indeed. The point is, although the essential goodness of life is trustworthy, not all specific *things* in life are trustworthy. Although God is trustworthy, not all of God's creation can be trusted to treat us kindly all the time. Although our essential nature is trustworthy, there are many ways in which we can fool ourselves. Blind, foolish trust is trusting in the specifics of life, not in the essential goodness within them. It is foolish to trust that a snake will not bite you or a scorpion not sting you. That does not mean the snake or the scorpion are bad creatures—only that they need to be treated with respect. Note carefully that wise trust is neither paranoid nor capricious; it has a quality of simple, open-eyed respect. All things and all people deserve such respect. Wise trust comes not from esoteric knowledge, but from keeping your eyes and ears open. We can learn some of this from the animals: watch how they become still and alert, how they sniff the air, how they perk up their ears, reading the signs, sifting the benevolent from the dangerous. Everything is in the noticing.

Wise trust comes through being alert to our present condition, and it also comes through being aware of our experience. It comes through making mistakes and learning from them. This is one of the harder facts of trust; we can't avoid getting hurt. Both emotionally and physically, we have been and will be injured by the experience of living. Wise trust, then, accepts that pain may come. It tries to avoid injury, but it is willing to endure pain if it is inevitable, and to learn from it. And then, with eyes and ears open, it takes the risk again.

When one lover hurts another, the one who is hurt may say "I'll never trust you again." What does this mean? If it means "I'll never trust you not to hurt me again," it is a wise statement; we cannot help hurting one another. If it means "I'll never love you again," it is foolish; to avoid loving to keep from being hurt is like trying to stop breathing so you won't catch a cold.

Wise trust, then, does not mean trusting that we'll always do the right thing or that we will never be hurt. It does not mean trusting that everyone and everything have our best interests at heart. It goes deeper than this. It is, as I say, fundamentally respectful. It recognizes that there is benevolence and danger in all creation and all creatures, including oneself. Grounded in fundamental respect, wise trust is courageous, willing to make mistakes, willing to be hurt because it knows there is an essential goodness beneath errors and pain, perhaps even *within* them. Wise trust chooses life, not protection. It sheds its armor so it can run free with clear eyes and open senses. It comes out of its burrow so it can play in the sunlight.

If we try to objectify trust too much, it is easy to reduce it to a purely psychological phenomenon. Some psychologists say that if we had most of our needs met in childhood, we will be more trusting in later life. At one level this may be true, but trust that comes from having only good experiences may not be so wise. Wise trust comes not from having everything go well for us, but from weathering storms and learning that we can survive. In this sense, trust seems much more a spiritual choice than a psychological trait. To be sure, some abused children grow into paranoid and paralyzed adults. But other abused children become truly courageous and wise. What makes the difference? What is it that enables any of us to keep going when things seem hopeless? For that matter, what allows some of us to learn from our mistakes while others just keep repeating them? There is something more than psychological determinism here, and something more than willpower.

I believe that what makes the difference is a combination of personal will and divine grace. It is a conscious act of will to choose life and love over fear and defense. But the empowerment to make such a choice in a particular situation is a gift, an act of grace. The two must come together: the gift and our acceptance of it, the invitation and our "yes" to it. This mysterious connection between human will and divine grace is the essence of spirituality.

SPIRITUALITY

Everyone has a spiritual life. Because spirituality refers to our deepest values and desires, the very core of our being, no one is exempt from it. We experience our spirituality in very different ways; some of us see it in religious terms, others in a more secular fashion. Some of us do our best to ignore it entirely. It would be safe to say that what any of us actually experi-

ence of our spirituality is only a superficial representation. We
are all part of a creation so vast and incomprehensible that our
most accurate perceptions can only be partial sketches, tiny
brief glimpses. There is no doubt of this; our religions have
been proclaiming it for millennia and our modern sciences are
demonstrating its truth. Whether we like it or not, we can no
longer expect to stand apart from creation and hope to comprehend it, much less control it. The only sane option is to consciously *join* the immense process of life of which we are always
and irrevocably a part. Anything else is delusion.

Americans will ask how to do this. How do we join the
process of life? Because we are already a part of things, the
joining is not really a doing at all. It is simply an interior admission or recognition, an acceptance, a gentle surrender, a willingness to begin each moment freshly. Sometimes, when we have
been struggling for control, the joining seems like we are saying
to ourselves "I am not the master of my destiny," and it is
accompanied by a feeling of relaxation, perhaps a sigh. At other
times, when we have been hiding out in self-protection, it is
like we are saying "O.K., let's see what the next moment
brings," and the feeling is one of expectancy, courage, willingness to take risks—a deep breath and a readiness to move
ahead. I am sure you know these feelings; they are nothing new.
I am trying to describe them a little because our culture still
does not give them much credibility even though they are the
most life-giving feelings of all. They mark our return from a
desperate, deluded striving for control to a stance of real integrity, of natural authenticity. Such feelings of joining with life or
rejoining oneself are signs of our spirituality finding freedom.

I have to say again, as I have so many times over the past
seventeen years, that there is no "how to" in this. If we are
willing for it, if we are open and awake to its possibility, it just
happens. It is given. My religious faith explains it thus: God is
endlessly, irrepressibly and unconditionally loving, always call-

ing us home. But in that love, God leaves us always free to accept or decline the invitation. God treats us with absolute respect. God may beckon us gently or challenge us fiercely, but God will not make us puppets and pull our strings. We may delude ourselves into thinking that we should control our lives and destinies, but God suffers no such delusion. Whoever or whatever God is, God is sane. Love does not control. Love frees.

RELIGION

Popular religion, like popular psychology, is likely to suggest "how to's" for achieving health and peace of mind. I am convinced that any such methods deny the active reality of God's love, which is grace. Further, they inevitably put God at an artificial distance from us. To think of God "out there, in charge of things," is to separate us from God's lively loving intimacy, the indwelling presence of the divine. To be sure, God is not simply ourselves and not just within us; in some way God is beyond everything. God *is* "out there," irrevocably other; if it were not so, there would be no possibility of relationship. At the same time, however, God is also "in here," immeasurably intimate—as the mystics say, closer to us than our very breath, closer even than we are to ourselves.

How, then, could we "do" something to approach this loving One who is so close? How could we get to the "place" where this One lives? The question itself is delusional. There is no place to go. We are already there. It is a matter of simply being open to what is, and, once we have seen what is, admitting it. This is simple sanity. It's right here, in front of your eyes, right now. It always is, always has been, always will be.

Regardless of our religious beliefs, the truth of our genuine spirituality will take us into some kind of relationship with the essential Source and Power of this great process of which we are a part. Some may feel it as a friendly, loving relationship. Others may approach it with suspicion or even hostility. Still others will do anything possible not to get involved. Yet we are involved and there is no way to avoid it. At the point of recognizing this relationship, our natural spirituality merges with religion. Religion offers structure, context and interpretation for spiritual existence. Just as everyone has a spiritual life, then, all of us who have reflected upon our spiritual lives have at least some kind of religion. Spirituality is given to us as part of our creation. Religion is our human response to that gift, our attempt to name and claim it, to appreciate it and live it as fully as possible. Among other things, religion allows us to name the Giver.

I don't pretend to know who God is. I've grown up with a Christian belief; the orthodoxy of Christianity fits my experience and Jesus challenges me more than I would ever wish for, so I guess I'm satisfied. You have to claim some kind of tradition if you're going to do much thinking about these things. But just as I'm sure of the endless love of God, I'm sure that no particular religion has exclusive rights to the one and only truth.

Not too long ago I received a letter from a man who had read the original paperback edition of *Simply Sane* after some of my other, more overtly "Christian" books. Not noticing the publication dates, he thought *Simply Sane* was my latest book. He was quite sure I had lost my faith and sold out to the Buddhists. Although he was decidedly upset with me, I was grateful for his response because he gave me the energy to come back and tackle this thing directly. I will never understand why religions based on love can so readily draw circles around themselves that exclude people who believe differently. Why can we not understand and accept that *none* of us really knows completely what we are talking about? I think of God speaking to Job, treating him with incredible respect but letting him know in no uncertain terms how it is. "Where were you when I created the heavens?" In other words, "Beloved child of mine, who do you think you are?"

We're all God's children; we're all *children*, and none of us has a special handle on the truth. If we can surrender the notion that we ought to be the ultimate masters of everything, the identity of children can be truly wonderful. Again, this is something all the world's great faiths proclaim. So I don't know who God is, and neither do you. Even to use the word "God" is to diminish the mysterious, intimate reality of that loving One who flows impeccably through our lives. Any name is inadequate. In this sense, it even seems irrelevant to me whether someone "believes in God." To "believe in God," at least in the popular sense, means to cling to some fixed image of who God is, and for most of us that would be idolatry. Whoever God is, God is simply too intimate and too beyond-us to fit into any of our images. We might as well accept it.

Like all other created things, religion needs to be approached with respect, with wise trust. It is both dangerous and good. It is dangerous in its capacity to over-explain the divine mystery and over-secure us by reducing grace to a how-to method. It can become literally deadly when it claims exclusive rights to the truth. Perhaps for reasons such as these, Martin Buber once said that he did not like religion very much and was very happy that the word did not appear anywhere in the Bible. But religion has deep goodness in it as well. Religion connects us with a great tradition of other people, people who have gone before us. It allows us access to their wisdom. It gives us a community of faith, a tradition of symbols, a shared language to work with, a source of inspiration and critique, and guidelines for living with one another.

It is probably unnecessary for me to be saying any of this; you already have your spirituality and you probably have your religion. You most likely even have your own good ways of being wise with it. I do however want to call you to sharpen your sensitivities and look beneath the surface. What is *real* for you in faith? What is your actual experience? Take a breath and face into your faith courageously, just as it is. See what is there. Feel what you desire. Sense where your doubts are. Own your certainties. Whether you can justify it or not, claim what you know as true. But claim it with gentleness, with flexibility. Do not freeze it. Let it be free to grow into ever deeper truth.

In my own faith, there are a few simple things of which I have become certain. First, although I don't know who or what God is, I have no doubt about God's existence. I'm happy that I don't know God's face; it allows God to come to me as God will. Second, I know God is loving and that God's loving is trustworthy. I know this directly, through the experience of my life. There have been plenty of times of doubt, especially when I used to believe that trusting God's goodness meant I would not be hurt. But having been hurt quite a bit, I know God's goodness goes deeper than all pleasure and pain—it embraces them both. Third, I know God responds to prayer. I don't know how or why; but I know it is true.

PRAYER

From the standpoint of human choice and intention, prayer is the fundamental way our spirituality expresses itself and through which wise trust comes to us. It is through prayer, in prayerfulness, that we become more authentically open and accurately responsive to who we are and the way life really is. I have chosen my words carefully here; prayer is the way through which we become more open to wise trust, not a method of achieving it. This distinction will become clearer as we look at prayer more precisely.

Many people think it is necessary to have some particular belief in God or image of God in order to pray. I am sure this is not true. I prayed before I had any sense or surety of God whatsoever; many of my friends did also. Many still do. Prayer, in its most basic honesty, is an utterly simple reaching out of the human heart, feeling its desires, its fears, its thankfulness, toward whatever power there may be at the foundation of life. True prayer is your honest expression of what you long for, what you hope for, what you most deeply feel. It doesn't have to be in words or images; it can just be a yearning. But it extends beyond yourself in the recognition that the whole weight of the universe cannot rest upon your shoulders alone.

My religious faith and personal experience both assure me that one does not have to have a completely correct or orthodox theology in order to pray. The good news is that God is close to us, already accepting our intimacy, and we do not have to have any degree of sophistication whatsoever to access God's love. This good news is not for the theologically correct any more than it is for the psychologically or politically correct. It is for everyone: the retarded, the "insane," the abused, the dysfunctional, the crippled, the hopeless, the homeless, even the theologians and gurus of our time. It could not be otherwise for a truly loving God.

I believe that in one way or another everybody prays. In Chapter 11 I gave some advice for people who do and don't pray. That was shorthand for people who do and don't *experience* prayer. Even from a secular standpoint, prayer happens naturally to all of us. It happens whenever our heart's desire reaches out beyond us: when we want something very badly, when we are very afraid, when we are deeply touched by beauty, when we fall in love, when we are overcome with gratitude. It happens at births and deaths, in times of crisis and great joy. Sometimes even our dreams are prayers.

Even if we think prayer is superstitious or immature, even if it embarrasses us, it still happens. We can't stop it. Psychology has long established that we have a psychic life that goes on all the time beneath our awareness. Part of that life is prayer. Many Christians interpret this as the Holy Spirit praying within us. Some mystics go even further, saying that all the intentional prayers we might offer are nothing more than attempts to join the continual unconscious prayer of that Spirit which never ceases in our hearts. However we may interpret it, prayer is as natural to human beings as smiling or crying. It happens in all cultures. The eighteenth-century poet James Montgomery wrote that prayer, uttered or unexpressed, is the soul's sincere desire. As such, prayer is part of who we are, so innate that we have to actively suppress it if we want to keep it out of our awareness. And even then, at some level, it still goes on.

From this perspective it is absurd to be told that we should pray, or how to pray, or that one kind of prayer is better than another. It's a bit like being told how to digest our food or grow our skin. It is even more absurd to look at prayer as a technique or a skill. The question is not whether you pray nor how nor even why. The only real question is how you *are* with your prayer. What is your attitude toward it, your respect for it, your comfort and honesty with it? Even this question is not one of judgement; there is no right or wrong to it.

When I suggest prayer, then, it means to *allow* prayer more freedom in your consciousness and life, to own it and appreciate it more deeply. Let me say it one more time: prayer itself is not a doing. It is part of who we are. There are many things we *can* do to give our prayer more freedom, to nurture an environment around and within us that supports the fullness of our prayer. We can take quiet time in little moments or long stretches. We can relax our bodies or attend to our breath. We can find or make places that help us pray. We can read scripture, listen to music, watch the sky, go to the woods. We can light a candle, sit before an icon, repeat holy words, join with others in worship. Such doings may assist the freedom of prayer or help our minds be more receptive and attentive to prayer, but none of them is prayer itself.

In a spiritual sense, prayer is a gift like all other given aspects of human nature. But conscious prayer is also exquisitely personal; it involves our choice, our will. Whenever we pray consciously—which is to say when we own our honest feelings and reach beyond ourselves, with them—we are also claiming a desire for connectedness with the source and essential power of life. This orientation, this attitude of reaching out or opening up beyond ourselves, is an essential characteristic of prayer; it is what separates prayer from self-absorption.

To summarize, I have described three fundamental qualities of prayer. First, it is a natural, ongoing part of who we are. Second, it is oriented beyond ourselves; it is always seeking or expressing some kind of connectedness. Third, whenever it becomes conscious it involves our will, our capacity for choice and intention. When our wills do become involved, a wide range of possibilities exists. At one extreme, we can deny or ignore our prayer altogether, try to put it out of our minds. At the opposite extreme, we can try to take it over and make it a technique that is wholly under our conscious control. It is at this extreme that prayer becomes superstitious, a means for trying to manipulate divine power. Somewhere in-between these extremes lies the possibility of allowing prayer to freely be just what it is, to let it be natural, honest and spontaneous. Here we "join" our prayer in the same way that spirituality involves joining with the deep true currents of our lives: consciously entering into life fully. In this sense, prayer and spirituality are inseparable. The simple sanity of prayer, as of life, is in participating enthusiastically with what is naturally given to us.

When we join with our inherent prayer in this way, we naturally move beyond just expressing our desires, fears and thankfulness. We become receptive as well as expressive. We begin to listen. We open to the possibility of something coming to us or arising within us. Most authentically, this emerging receptivity happens not because we think it should, not because it is the right way to pray, but simply because it is a natural aspect of prayer that grows as we allow it.

WISDOM

It is in this more receptive, listening, perceptive dimension of prayer that we are most available to wise trust. Wisdom comes to us where we are attentive, sensitive, open to it. Occasionally it comes to us in little packages: sudden insights, "Aha!" experiences, flashes of intuition, special realizations. More often, though, it seems to flow within us like an underground stream, nourishing us in a subterranean way, beneath our intellectual understanding. It may even come to us as a sense of *presence,* as if a wise and caring companion were accompanying us.

In many deep faith traditions, wisdom is seen as just such a companion. Ancient Egyptian and Hebrew religions often portrayed wisdom as a feminine personification of the divine, an active, living manifestation of God. The feminine presence of wisdom was *Hokmah* to the Jews, as in the first chapter of Proverbs: "Wisdom cries out in the streets, she raises her voice in the public squares." In Greek, her name was *Sophia,* as in the Gospel renderings of Jesus' words "Wisdom is justified of her children." Another translation says she is "justified by her actions." In much of mystical literature, Wisdom is a feminine presence of God who draws us, beckons us, and shows us the way toward deeper communion with the divine One.

Such images of wisdom may be helpful in understanding or deepening our experience, but as with all our images of world, self and God, they are not the reality they represent.

Their fundamental value, I think, is in emphasizing that wisdom is far more than an achievement of human intelligence. It is a power and a presence *given* to us, coming to us, arising within us, providing guidance as we grope for our hearts' deepest desire. From a practical standpoint this means we find wisdom not by skillfully using our intellects but by opening our senses, listening, becoming receptive and attentive to what might be being given. Wisdom may indeed be crying out in the streets, but to hear her we need to stop and listen; we need to have "ears to hear."

Perhaps I have already made it too complex with all these words and images. Earlier I encouraged us to learn from the animals, how they pause, perk up their ears, open their senses. Now I am simply connecting that attentiveness with the receptive quality of prayer. It is not a connection that we have to make. It happens naturally. And as it does, we begin to live prayerfully.

PRAYERFULNESS

I have described prayer as a deep current of self-expression and receptivity that is always going on within us. Praying, as a conscious act, is simply a matter of attending to this interior expression and receptivity: honestly being ourselves with whatever true feelings and desires we have, and being open to things as they really are. As such, conscious prayer need not be restricted to any particular times or places. If we are given just a little space, just a brief opportunity, the qualities of prayer can emerge anywhere and at any time, in the midst of whatever situation we may be in. As they emerge, we become prayer*full*. We begin to live a prayerful life.

Prayerfulness is a quality of presence, a manner of being, an attitude. We always approach the situations of our lives with some kind of attitude. We might be suspicious, trusting, hopeful, optimistic, defensive, bored, antagonistic, or any of a host of other possibilities. To be precise, an attitude is something like a chosen mood, a coloration of awareness with which we greet our experience. Most often our attitudes are habitual or reflexive and quite superficial. For example, when I enter a situation where I have been hurt in the past, I am likely to have a defensive, mistrusting attitude. If I maintain that attitude, I will not be very open to good things that might happen; I may even fulfill my own prophecy by contributing to the negativity of the situation. Similarly, if I maintain an overly optimistic attitude simply because everything has gone well in the past, I may be blindly trusting. Either way, attitudes generally color and restrict our receptivity to the immediate realities of situations.

But what if we could choose a prayerful attitude? What if we could enter situations prayerfully and remain prayerful within them? As I have described prayerfulness, this would mean simply yet fully being who we are, very present to the real situation as it is, and at the same time gently, naturally open to that which is beyond and within ourselves and the situation. To pick it apart this way makes it sound rather complicated, and so it would be if we tried to make it happen. Again we must remember that prayerfulness is *natural*. It is something to be allowed rather than achieved.

It took me a long time to learn this. For many years I tried to *do* it. I tried to "pray constantly," to "practice the presence," to "be contemplative." The effort was very frustrating because I was trying to impose something upon myself when what I wanted was inside me all the time, simply wanting the freedom to express itself. I don't know how I learned the lesson; I'm not even sure I have learned it that well yet. But surely my repeated failures at trying so hard have taught me something. I also think wilderness solitude helped me. There is something about the "is-ness" of nature—the way trees just are trees and the way animals just simply do their animal things—that demonstrates how we human beings are also meant to be. However it has happened, I am certain that what little I know of prayerful living has been Wisdom's gift. To put it another way, just as trust grows through trusting, prayerfulness comes through praying. And it all weaves together in slowly emerging patterns: prayerfulness, trust, wisdom, love, prayerfulness . . .

With all these words of elaboration, I can now re-recommend my suggestions in Chapter 11 for when you pray, when you don't pray, and when you can't pray. We will just understand, with a little smile, that prayer is happening in spite of us, no matter what.

INTERCESSION

I want to reiterate my belief that authentic prayer and prayerfulness are not really means to any particular ends. If I am sick or distressed, my prayer may naturally be for healing. That is honest prayer, the expression of my condition and desire. But it is not something I do *in order to* be healed. It is not a method, technique or procedure. The same understanding must apply to all kinds of prayer, even to intercessory prayer for others. In praying for others we express our honest desire for their well-being. But it is not the broadcast of a spiritual energy beam, bouncing off an angelic satellite to hit its target with waves of healing power. Having said this, I must also say I am convinced that honest prayer does make a difference. Petition, prayer for ourselves, really helps us. I know from experience that intercessory prayer is absolutely helpful for others. And prayers of thanksgiving, praise and love are, I am sure, truly helpful to God. It is one of God's tricks on us that while prayer "works," we can't "do" it that way.

Logically, all this is a paradox. There are many good works on the theology of prayer, but those that are truly good always come back to an affirmation of its fundamental mystery. Logic is a wonderful tool for helping us understand something of ourselves and of the world, but the essential nature of things simply will not fit inside logic. This is but one of the reasons why wisdom is so different from knowledge, why wise trust is so unlike calculated certainty, why prayer, like our very selves, refuses to be objectified. Here again there may be some real value in a childlike kind of presence, a knowing-that-we-don't-know. If we try to know too much, we will waste time and miss opportunities for simple appreciation. If we think we know too much, we will be deluding ourselves. It seems to me that anything that really *needs* to be understood about life has to be understood by the least sophisticated or intelligent of us—which means there probably isn't all that much that we really have to understand.

Given our desire and willingness—and gentleness of touch—our prayer will emerge into consciousness as part of our natural being, an expression of who we are. As it does so, it will not be solely self-centered. It will not be narcissistic. It will reach out with our love and care to embrace the world. I think it is very good to notice this emergence, to appreciate and welcome it, but I do not think we need to control it in any way. To use an analogy from the old text, our prayer, like our sanity, emerges from underground in the manner of a plant in springtime. If we check it too much or try to pull it this way or that, we will not be helping its growth. As with everything fundamental to ourselves, we would do well to be very gentle.

GENTLENESS

In all my experience as a psychiatrist and as a human being, the deepest, most pervasive pathology I have seen is the incredible harshness we have towards ourselves. I don't know where it comes from originally, but I know it is at the core of so many of our troubles. We jerk ourselves around, berate ourselves, drive ourselves and confine ourselves in ways we would never subject an animal to. We are willing subjects of our own abuse. The most religious of us are so terrified of appearing selfish that we subject ourselves to unnamable internal cruelties. And those of us who *are* more selfish stuff ourselves with poisons and whip ourselves into self-destructive highs. Some of us are meaner than others, but I have yet to meet a person in modern western culture who was not in some way cruelly self-abusive.

I say I do not know the origin of our self-persecution, but I can't help having some ideas about it. For some of us, there is no doubt that religious education has been a culprit. In Christianity, for example, the notion that human beings are fundamentally bad, recipients of original sin, has been drummed into both children and adults for centuries. Religious condemnation and moral guilt have been used for child-rearing and political control. In less religious settings, shame and fear have been found to be effective weapons for child-control. I wonder, does the whole thing have to do with control? Is it that we are so convinced that we must control ourselves, and so frustrated by not being able to, that we turn on ourselves and on our children in spite, snapping and gnawing at our own flesh like animals caught in a trap?

In my opinion, our mania for child-building and self-fixing is just another expression of our cruelty towards ourselves. It was the ancient Roman playwright Terence who first said that charity begins at home. Cruelty does also. After working with persons convicted of repeated crimes of violence, I am firmly convinced that cruelty toward others has its roots in cruelty towards oneself. It is now common knowledge that most child abusers were abused as children themselves, but I am speaking of a deeper level where we abuse ourselves. Somehow we learn it, somehow it becomes entrenched within us, and somehow it becomes contagious. It is no accident that our society is so violent externally and simultaneously so prone to self-persecution. The more cruel we are to ourselves, the more likely we are to be mean to others.

There is a popular psychological theory that we need to take care of ourselves first, that we need to reclaim our own sense of personal worth and dignity before we can act on the second great commandment: love your neighbor as yourself. I do not agree with this completely because I know it is possible to be kind to others even if you feel terrible about yourself. But I would suggest that if we want a more loving life, we do need to be a whole lot gentler towards ourselves.

Like the rest of nature, human beings have inherent capacities for benevolence and cruelty, for beauty and danger. Nonproductive violence and needless cruelty are present throughout the animal world. It is a mistaken myth that human beings are the only creatures who kill or torture for pleasure; cats do it, birds do it, chimpanzees do it, many if not most animals do it. We are no exception in this regard, and therefore we need to treat ourselves as we need to treat the wilderness: with respect, with wise trust. But there is something cultural about our unique brutalities, and especially about the extent to which we brutalize ourselves. Such self-persecution is not common to all cultures. There are gentler societies than ours, and they are not so interested in controlling things. They show us by their example that as human beings we do have the capacity to live more gently.

Without pursuing all the anthropological and theological nuances of self-cruelty, let me suggest something very, very simple. You know what tenderness is. We all have experiences of gentleness and kindness. Think of something that makes you feel that way: perhaps being with a loved one who is suffering, or seeing a small child asleep—whatever calls forth from you a feeling of warmth and tenderness or just simple caring. Feel that feeling. You can do that, almost without trying. It is a very familiar feeling, well known to you. Can you now, just for a moment, feel that way towards yourself?

I am not encouraging you to try to maintain a steady state of self-love, but simply to bring a little kindness toward yourself from time to time. Just an instant of it, just a brief interior touch. This is what gentleness means, and it is in this good atmosphere that your basic sanity can grow. The feeling of kindness towards yourself will probably disappear quickly and be replaced by some old, harsh rigidity. That is all right. When you think of it again, when it again is possible, you can recall it. For God's sake, do not throw upon yourself the extra burden of "having" to feel kindly toward yourself. It's just in the moment, just in the instant, a little touch of gentleness, like a feather.

Not long ago the Dalai Lama came to Washington, D.C., and spoke about compassion. A man so erudite, so sophisticated in the ways of the spirit and the world might be expected to have given a very complex description of his subject. In fact, he called compassion "warm feeling."

Can you, from time to time, just nurture a little warm feeling towards yourself? I truly believe that's all it takes. A little warm feeling creates an atmosphere of acceptance, of allowing, of permitting. And within that atmosphere there is a kind of encouragement for the goodness to grow: the goodness that is you, the goodness that is life in you, the goodness of creation in you, God's goodness in you.

It doesn't take mastery. It doesn't take sophistication. It doesn't take anything other than your own simple truthful desire for life and love and goodness. After all, it all, still, just simply is.